2

ALSO BY BOBBY FLAY

Bobby Flay's Boy Gets Grill: 125 Reasons to Light Your Fire!
(with Julia Moskin)

Bobby Flay Cooks American: Great Regional Recipes with Sizzling New Flavors
(with Julia Moskin)

Bobby Flay's Boy Meets Grill: With More Than 125 Bold New Recipes
(with Joan Schwartz)

Bobby Flay's From My Kitchen to Your Table
(with Joan Schwartz)

Bobby Flay's Bold American Food
(with Joan Schwartz)

BOBBY FLAY'S
GRILLING FOR LIFE

75 HEALTHIER IDEAS FOR BIG FLAVOR FROM THE FIRE

BOBBY FLAY

with Stephanie Banyas

and Sally Jackson

Foreword by Joy Bauer, MS, RD, CDN

Color Photographs by Gentl & Hyers

Black-and-White Photographs by John Dolan

Scribner

New York   London   Toronto   Sydney

SCRIBNER
1230 Avenue of the Americas
New York, NY 10020

SCRIBNER and design are trademarks of Macmillan Library Reference USA, Inc.,
used under license by Simon & Schuster, the publisher of this work.

For information about special discounts for bulk purchases,
please contact Simon & Schuster Special Sales:
1-800-456-6798 or business@simonandschuster.com

DESIGNED BY ERICH HOBBING

Text set in Rockwell

Manufactured in the United States of America

10 9 8 7 6 5 4 3 2 1

Library of Congress Control Number: 2005045053

ISBN 0-7432-7272-2

*This book is dedicated
to Sophie and Stephanie,
who encourage me to make
healthy choices every day of my life.*

Acknowledgments

Stephanie Banyas

Sally Jackson

Beth Wareham

Rica Allannic

Jane Dystel

John Fulbrook

John Dolan

Gentl & Hyers

Neil Manacle

Laurence Kretchmer

Jerry Kretchmer

Jeff Bliss

Stephanie March

Dorothy Flay

Bill Flay

The staffs of Mesa Grill NY, Bolo, and Mesa Grill Las Vegas

Food Network

CBS's *The Early Show*

Contents

Foreword   xiii

Introduction   3

Equipment   7

Fahrenheit 101   11

Herbs and Spices   13

Flavorings   21

How to . . .   25

VEGETABLES   **29**

Grilled Asparagus and Egg Salad with Tarragon-Caper Vinaigrette   30

Grilled Antipasto with Gorgonzola Vinaigrette   32

Grilled and Marinated Zucchini and Yellow Squash   34

Grilled Asian-Style Eggplant Salad   36

Grilled Zucchini Succotash   38

Grilled Fennel and Orange Salad with Almonds and Mint   40

Grilled German Sweet Potato Salad   42

Grilled Sweet Potato Salad with Pancetta and Rosemary Vinaigrette   44

Grilled Portobello Mushrooms Stacked with Spinach and Manchego Cheese   46

Red Cabbage and Beet Slaw   48

Bulgur Salad with Green Onion Vinaigrette   50

Grilled Spice-Rubbed Vidalia Onions   52

Twice-Grilled Peppers with Buffalo Mozzarella and Caper-Basil Vinaigrette   54

Grilled New Potatoes with Lemon-Garlic Aïoli and Chives   56

Pickled Jalapeños   58

FISH AND SHELLFISH   61

Buckwheat Pizza with Cilantro Pesto, Jack Cheese, and Grilled Shrimp   62

Garlic–Red Chile–Thyme–Marinated Shrimp   66

Grilled Prawns with Spicy Fresh Pepper Sauce   68

Greek Orzo and Grilled Shrimp Salad with Mustard-Dill Vinaigrette   70

Grilled Shrimp Escabeche   72

Grilled Shrimp in Lettuce Leaves with Serrano-Mint Sauce   74

Grilled Clams on the Half-Shell with Bacon, Garlic, and Hot Pepper   76

Grilled Oysters with Mango Pico de Gallo and Red Chile Horseradish   78

Cumin Grilled Sea Scallops with Chickpea Salad and Red Pepper–Tahini Vinaigrette   80

Grilled Sea Scallops with Avocado Vinaigrette and Jalapeño Pesto   84

Grilled Lobster Tails with Hot Ginger–Green Onion Vinaigrette   86

"Barbecued" Mahimahi with Yellow Pepper–Cilantro Pesto   88

Grilled Halibut with Grilled Eggplant Salad   90

Yucatán Marinated Halibut in Banana Leaves with Pineapple-Orange Relish   92

Grilled Jerk-Rubbed Grouper with Hot Vinegar Sauce   94

Grilled Red Snapper with Grapefruit-Thyme Mojo   96

Grilled Red Snapper with Green Romesco Sauce   98

Grilled Salmon with Anchovy Vinaigrette and Grilled Pepper and Black Olive Relish   100

Grilled Salmon with Lemon, Dill, and Caper Vinaigrette   102

Whole Sea Bass with Charred Serrano–Basil Vinaigrette   104

Grilled Brook Trout with Horseradish and Tarragon Tartar Sauce   106

Grilled Tuna with White Bean Salad   108

Grilled Tuna Salad Sandwiches with Lemon-Habanero Mayonnaise   110

Grilled Tuna with Fennel-Tomatillo Relish   112

Grilled Tuna Burgers with Green Onion Mayonnaise and Watercress   114

Tuna au Poivre Salad with Creamy Tarragon-Garlic Vinaigrette   116

POULTRY   119

Grilled Chicken Cutlets with Lemon and Black Pepper and
   Arugula-Tomato Salad   120

Grilled Chicken Breasts with Fontina and Prosciutto with Sage-Orange
   Vinaigrette   122

Grilled Chicken Breasts Stuffed with Goat Cheese with Green
   Chile–Cilantro Sauce   124

Chinese Chicken Salad with Red Chile–Peanut Dressing   126

Spanish-Spiced Chicken with Mustard–Green Onion Sauce   128

Grilled Chicken Tenders with Spicy Chipotle Sauce and Blue
   Cheese–Yogurt Sauce   130

Grilled Turkey Burgers with Monterey Jack, Poblano Pickle Relish,
   and Avocado Mayonnaise   132

Grilled Turkey Cutlets with Sage-Lemon Pesto   134

Bricked Rosemary Chicken with Lemon   136

Balsamic-Thyme-Glazed Duck Breasts   138

Grilled Duck Breast with Black Pepper–Sweet Mustard Sauce   140

PORK, BEEF, AND LAMB   143

Pork Tenderloin Crusted with Green Onion, Jalapeño, and Ginger   144

Grilled Fennel-Spiced Pork Chops with Sage-Lemon Vinaigrette   146

Pork Satay with Red Chile–Peanut Sauce and Napa Cabbage–Green
   Onion Slaw   148

Espresso-Rubbed BBQ Ribs with Mustard-Vinegar Basting Sauce   151

Garlic-Mustard-Grilled Beef Skewers   154

Green Chile Burgers   156

Black Pepper–Crusted Filet Mignon with Goat Cheese and Roasted Red
   Pepper–Ancho Salsa   158

Grilled Beef Filet with Arugula and Parmesan   160

Grilled T-Bone Steaks with Garlic-Chile Oil   162

Red Wine–Rosemary–Marinated Flank Steak with Lemony White Beans   164

Smoky and Fiery Skirt Steak with Avocado-Oregano Relish 166

Harissa-Marinated Lamb Skewers on Farro Salad with Pine Nuts
and Goat Cheese 168

Grilled Lamb Chops and Oregano Vinaigrette with Radish Tzatziki 170

Lamb Burgers with Tomato-Mint Salsa and Feta Cheese 172

Souvlaki with Merguez Sausage and Piquillo Pepper–Yogurt Sauce 174

Yogurt-Mint-Marinated Grilled Leg of Lamb 178

DRINKS AND DESSERTS **181**

Cantaloupe-Mint Agua Fresca (Mexican Fruit Cooler) 182

Green Tea Mint Iced Tea 183

Pomegranate Margarita 184

White Nectarine Bellini 185

Grilled Apricots with Bittersweet Chocolate and Almonds 186

Strawberries with Ricotta Cream 187

Grilled Plums with Spiced Walnut-Yogurt Sauce 188

Grilled Figs with Vanilla-Orange Crème Fraîche and Toasted Pistachios 190

Mix and Match 193

Meals in Minutes 195

Party Foods 197

Sources 199

Index 201

Foreword

When Bobby Flay asked me to work with him on his next cookbook, I was thrilled! I'm a huge fan of his restaurants and television shows and was ecstatic to hear that a great chef was also interested in healthy eating. Bobby's food is renowned for its bold flavor, and my task was to take his art and apply the science of nutrition. He was particularly interested in carbohydrates—eliminating the bad and incorporating the good. The resulting recipes are carb-healthy and packed with all the excitement that is the hallmark of Bobby's cooking.

As a nutritionist who owns two of New York's largest nutrition centers, I meet with people every day. Some just want to lose ten pounds, while others have been referred by physicians who specialize in everything from pediatrics to sports medicine. And if there is one category that confuses most everyone, it's carbohydrates. They believe that "watching their carb intake" means consuming lots of protein, swearing off potatoes and bread, and thinking nothing of chugging fruit juice and sweetening their oatmeal with honey.

Well, all carbs are not created equal. Simple carbohydrates—sugars of all colors—are all considered *bad* carbs and should certainly be limited. Unfortunately, simple carbohydrates are in everything from bottled barbecue sauce to commercial fruit juice, and because these sugars are practically already broken down into the form the body can utilize, they raise blood sugar levels too high, too quickly. While white, refined products aren't considered simple carbohydrates, they also rapidly convert into sugar after ingestion, causing sugar spikes and then subsequent crashes. These "swings" sap your physical and mental energy, not to mention what they can do to your weight.

What you want are the *good* carbs—complex carbohydrates that provide ample nutrition. They are nutrient-rich, high-fiber vegetables; whole grain foods; beans; and fresh fruits that are crucial to a healthy diet, reducing the risk of everything from cardiovascular disease to diabetes and cancer. These good carbs break down more slowly in the body, allowing you to maintain a constant energy level throughout the day. They also provide essential nutrients and help you feel fuller longer, and that's critical for achieving and maintaining a healthy weight.

None of the recipes in this book contains more than 10 percent of its total calories from simple sugars and refined carbs; and if the sugar content of a recipe exceeds 10 percent, it's from naturally occurring sugars found in healthy nutritious foods, such as low-fat dairy products, fresh fruits, and certain vegetables.

In addition to information about carbohydrates and sugar content, you'll find breakdowns for calories, total and saturated fat, cholesterol, protein, sodium, and fiber. To ensure nutritional accuracy, our analyses include only the amount of marinade, sauce, and dressing actually *consumed* in one serving. Pay close attention to the numbers if you have a medical condition that necessitates it. Watch the calories if weight loss is your concern. If you are on a low-salt diet because of high blood pressure, simply eliminate the added salt or decrease the amount you use in a recipe.

Some recipes are higher in saturated fat than others (especially those that feature red meat and whole milk cheese), so you might want to reserve these for special occasions. For those of you who watch your saturated fat intake for medical reasons, turn to the poultry and fish dishes in this book.

As for the rest of us, approach these nutritional analyses through the filter of common sense. If you have a heavy lunch, balance it out with a light supper lower in calories and fat.

A few other health notes: As I analyzed these recipes, I noticed that many are chock-full of disease-busting ingredients. For example, chile peppers, which Bobby uses a lot of, contain capsaicin—a chemical that stimulates circulation and acts as a safe, natural appetite suppressant. Olive oil is another wonder food found in many of these dishes. A monounsaturated fat, olive oil helps lower LDL ("bad") cholesterol while maintaining or increasing HDL ("good") cholesterol. The grilled salmon recipes in these pages are my absolute favorites because they're low in saturated fat, loaded with protein, and packed with omega-3 fats, which are found naturally in fish oils and benefit coronary health.

On behalf of the carb-phobic and the total-versus-saturated-fat-confused everywhere, I thank you, Bobby Flay. These good-carb, great-taste recipes offer health *and* flavor.

Healthfully yours,
Joy Bauer, MS, RD, CDN

BOBBY FLAY'S
GRILLING FOR LIFE

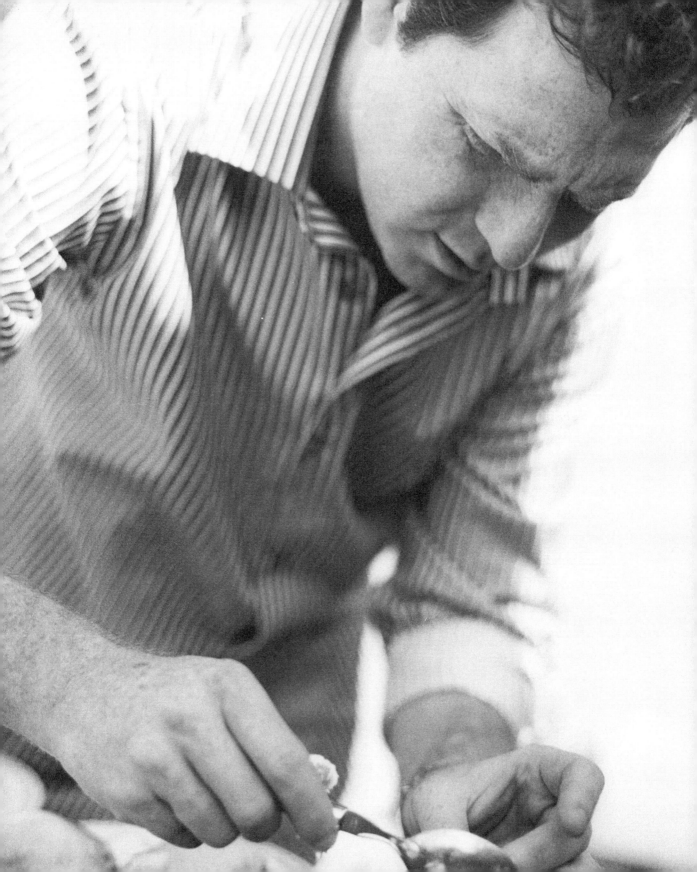

Introduction

First things first: I am not a nutritionist. I am a chef. I am not looking to create a new diet fad. Nor am I trying to jump on somebody else's bandwagon. What I am looking to do is to show how a healthy lifestyle can be enhanced by delicious meals from the grill. And this isn't just any food, for there are plenty of diet books and magazines with nutritionally sound (and a lot of bland) recipes out there already. This is the food that people want to eat—exciting, full of flavor—and it just so happens that you can make all of it while keeping within the guidelines of many of the current popular diets. Modifying the way you eat doesn't mean that you shouldn't really enjoy your food or that you can't feel proud to serve it to family and friends. I could never put a dish on the table that I didn't feel met both of those standards.

I'm not talking no carbs or low carbs, nonfat or low-fat. I am talking about the *right* carbs, the *right* fats. I can't write a book about something I don't believe in. I have always been a supporter of all things in moderation, and this book has nothing but heart and body healthy choices all the way.

You would have to be living under a rock not to have noticed the carbohydrate-cutting diets that have flooded the media and, in turn, totally changed the way Americans eat. I haven't spent one night in the kitchen of one of my restaurants in the past year without someone sending back the breadbasket or saying "No potatoes with that steak!" So I did a little research. And I think that some of these diets may be on to something—up to a point. But when I looked at the low-carb products and recipes out there—the revised breads, the barbecue sauces—I knew that I could never cook or eat that way. Soy flour may have its place, but it's not in my kitchen. And Splenda—what is that? Beyond the taste, it's just not natural. Sucralose (the base of Splenda) is a chlorocarbon. I'm not eating chlorine.

I can make some adjustments, but this can't be about substitutions. Too many recipes out there advocate the use of fake, processed food. I care too much about taste (among other things) to do that. I believe in purity of flavor. I'm not going to use sugar substitutes or imitation anything, but I do present a variety of dishes that will fit perfectly with today's carb-conscious lifestyle.

Healthy grilling seems too simple to even need a book. Maybe you think that grilling is nothing more than a hunk of meat tossed on the grill. But if you know anything about me and the way I cook, you know that I can never leave it at that. I want taste! I want excitement! I'll show you how to take your proteins from basic to outstanding without using the unwanted carbs found in many of today's prepared sauces and marinades. I think that the grill is the perfect instrument for preparing healthy, flavorful food. The grill, however, isn't the true focus of this book. Well-balanced and delicious food is. So go ahead and use a charcoal grill, a gas grill, a grill pan on the stove, or pop something under the broiler. In this instance, I think it's fair to say that how you cook is less important than what you cook.

And this book is not all meat—no way! I believe that we need a full and balanced diet to be happy and healthy. Like I said earlier, it's all about making the right choices with the right foods, all without overloading on artery-clogging fats. Heart-healthy oils like olive and canola, omega-3-rich fish like salmon, tons of veggies chock-full of fiber—they are all in here. I wanted to include some fantastic complex carbohydrates, too, with grilled buckwheat flatbread, salads with great grains like farro and bulgur, and whole-grain bread as the base for my sandwiches and burgers. Not only are they delicious, but complex carbohydrates are also so good for you—they fight heart disease and are slower to break down in your body, leaving you feeling fuller longer.

I have a signature style, and I want to demonstrate how that style can be used to enhance the flavors of all of your carb-conscious favorites and show you the way to a few new ones. And, yes, I might have to make some modifications to reduce carb intake. But remember, it will still be all about flavor! I would never do anything less.

I set out to write this book because I felt that people were getting too caught up in this crazy, carbless nonfat world. I believe that we should be able to eat everything—in reasonable portions. That being said, I wanted to find a way to bring good nutritious foods—and especially good carbs—back into the mix, while keeping my emphasis on flavor. I have definitely made concessions in order to keep the numbers in check, but this is not a low-calorie, low-fat, low-sodium book. There are many recipes in here that do meet those standards, and if you are eating by the numbers, you should be able to find quite a few options. I don't know anyone who wants to eat a big steak or lobster with butter every night of the week, and you shouldn't. Remember—moderation! That also means, however, there should be a time to indulge. I've made space for those indulgences. Don't cut out all carbs or fats; just pick the right ones. Don't indulge in heavy food every night; know when to celebrate with a special meal. I promise you can do it all, and with more flavor than you ever imagined. Just start with some good carb grilling!

Stuff newspaper into the bottom of the chimney starter.

Set the chimney starter right side up on a flat, heat-proof surface.

For charcoal, I prefer hardwood lump charcoal.

Fill to the top with charcoal.

Light the newspaper.

Heat the coals until they are covered with gray ash, then transfer them to your grill.

Equipment

Grilling is the most basic method of cooking there is. It dates back to the time of cave men—food plus fire equals good. So those are your two essential elements, your grill and your ingredients. But there are a few other things that you need to refine your grilling (and eating) experience. Make sure that you have the *right* ingredients, the *right* equipment and, of course, the *right* recipe.

I'll supply you with the recipes. As for equipment, my advice is to keep it simple. I don't buy into all those fancy grill tools. My checklist is basic, but it covers all you need for success on the grill. Here's what I recommend:

- **GRILL** I use both charcoal and gas, and both have their advantages. Whatever grill you choose, keep the grate reasonably clean, not crusted over.

    Gas is easy to light, control, and clean. A powerful gas grill provides strong heat and consistent temperatures. You can also easily adjust the temperature at any time during cooking, which is a bonus. There are several popular manufacturers of gas grills, and they are more expensive than charcoal, starting at several hundred dollars and reaching into the stratosphere.

    Charcoal is a lot more work, but it gives food a smokiness that gas can never imitate. Charcoal also provides an extremely hot fire, though it may take quite a bit of time to get it to that point. Should charcoal be your choice, you will find that even the top grills are reasonably priced. Look for a sturdy grill with a cover and a large grilling surface and, if possible, an adjustable grate and firebox. If you are going with a charcoal grill, don't use instant-light charcoal or lighter fluid—is that really what you want your food to taste like? Take the extra ten minutes and use a chimney starter for your coal (I like lump hardwood best) instead.

- **CHIMNEY STARTER** The single most important piece of equipment ever invented for the charcoal grill. If you are using charcoal, there is no excuse not to have one of these. There is no need to use lighter fluid again. Ever! (See page 6 for step-by-step instruction on how to use.)

- **HEAVY-DUTY GRILL BRUSH** It's really important to keep your grill clean, for baked-on food can completely ruin the taste of your dish. It's easiest to do with one of these brushes. Scrub the grate while the grill is still warm.

- **BRUSHES** are indispensable for applying glazes, sauces, and oils. You can buy pastry brushes, but I find that a paintbrush from the hardware store works just as well for much less money—which is good because the brushes can be hard to clean and need to be replaced frequently.

- **TONGS** are a piece of equipment that I can't grill without. I use them for picking up, turning, and moving just about everything on the grill—except for whole fish and delicate fish fillets. Don't waste your time with those extra-long grilling tongs normally found in the BBQ section of your local home-improvement store. They keep you at arm's length from your grill; get intimate and opt for the regular stainless-steel tongs in the housewares section of most large retail stores.

Cleaning the grate of a grill with a heavy-duty grill brush.

Brushing chicken breasts with glaze.

Using tongs to turn asparagus on the grill.

- **FISH SPATULA/HEAVY-DUTY METAL SPATULA** These have a wider and longer metal base than regular spatulas, which makes them perfect for sliding underneath food so that you can carefully turn whole fish and burgers without them falling apart.

- **MEAT THERMOMETER** Until you have the "touch test" down (pressing meat or fish with your finger to gauge the level of doneness), a thermometer is your best bet for making sure that meat and fish are cooked to the proper temperature. (See Fahrenheit 101, page 11.)

- **ELECTRIC COFFEE GRINDER** You should always have two: one for your coffee and one for your spices. Toasting (page 26) and grinding your own spices makes such a big difference in taste, and this piece of equipment makes the grinding part simple to do.

- **SQUEEZE BOTTLES** These inexpensive plastic bottles are perfect for storing sauces, oils, and vinaigrettes and adding splashes of color to your plate à la Jackson Pollock. They also allow you to control the amount of dressing you put on sal-

ipping burgers with a heavy-
uty metal spatula.

Checking the temperature with a meat thermometer.

ads and other dishes, and that's a good thing when you are counting calories. You can pick these up at restaurant supply stores as well as kitchen and housewares stores.

- **WHITE TERRY CLOTH TOWELS** Also known as bar towels, I use these by the dozen when I grill. They are a perfect substitute for bulky potholders, for cleaning off the edges of serving plates, and keeping your workspace clean as you go.

Using a squeeze bottle to sauce scallops.

Wiping a plate clean with a white terry cloth towel.

Fahrenheit 101

The second most common question I get asked (after what brand of grill I recommend) is what internal temperature should poultry, pork, beef, lamb, and fish be cooked to? The following "introductory" chart contains the internal temperatures that I prefer meat and fish to reach on an instant-read thermometer. The temperatures I list are the internal temperature at which meat/fish should be taken off the grill and the temperature at which it should be served after resting. All meat/fish should rest, loosely covered with foil to keep it warm, for at least 5 minutes after grilling to redistribute the juices and finish cooking; during this time the internal temperature of the meat will increase by 5 to 10 degrees.

The temperatures in this chart, in my opinion, keep the integrity of the meat and fish, meaning that when you cut into your meat it will be pink and juicy, not gray and dry. Fish should be moist and should flake when you break it apart with a fork. Nothing is worse than overcooked meat and fish. Why spend all that money only to be left with something resembling a piece of leather on your plate? I am also including the USDA recommendation for internal temperature, which tends to be 10 to 15 degrees higher than my recommendation and should be followed if you are feeding seniors, young children, pregnant women, or anyone with an illness or a weak immune system.

Beef Steaks/Lamb Chops: Medium-rare

Remove from heat	Serving temperature after resting	USDA recommends
130 degrees F	135 to 140 degrees F	150 degrees F

Ground Beef/Lamb: Medium

Remove from heat	Serving temperature after resting	USDA recommends
135 degrees F	140 to 145 degrees F	160 degrees F

Pork Tenderloin/Chops: Medium-well

Remove from heat	Serving temperature after resting	USDA recommends
145 degrees F	150 to 155 degrees F	170 degrees F

Chicken Breast/Turkey Breast: Medium-well

Remove from heat	Serving temperature after resting	USDA recommends
150 to 155 degrees F	160 degrees F	170 degrees F

Duck Breast: Medium-rare

Remove from heat	Serving temperature after resting	USDA recommends
135 degrees F	145 degrees F	170 degrees F

Fish Fillets/Whole Fish: Medium
(red snapper, halibut, salmon, mahimahi, and trout)

Remove from heat	Serving temperature after resting	USDA recommends
135 degrees F	140 to 145 degrees F	160 degrees F

Tuna: Medium-rare

Remove from heat	Serving temperature after resting	USDA recommends
120 degrees F	125 degrees F	160 degrees F

Herbs and Spices

Herbs and spices play a huge role in my cooking. Not only do they add incredible depth and complexity to my recipes, but they also do it without added fat, sugar, sodium or calories, which hide in many glazes and sauces, and that includes BBQ. You have some chicken slathered in commercial sauce, and an hour later you want to sell your soul for a candy bar. The hidden sugar in that sauce has set your craving into gear. But cutting down the sugar does not mean you have to cut out flavor. I make sure that I add plenty of fresh, bold flavor to my food by using tons of fresh herbs and spices. I prefer the flavor of fresh herbs, but there are a few instances, as with rubs, where dried are acceptable.

Spices should be bought whole whenever possible and ground in an electric coffee grinder just before using for optimal flavor. You could use a mortar and pestle to crush them and achieve this flavor as well. Dried spices begin to lose their flavor almost immediately after being ground, so buy spices whole and store them, tightly covered, in a cool, dark place.

Below is a brief overview of some of the herbs and spices I cook with most often. The best way to learn about herbs and spices is to cook with them. I hope the list along with the recipes in this book encourage you to experiment.

HERBS

- **Basil**—Basil brings a burst of sweet, minty flavor to most dishes. Basil should always be used fresh; when used dried, the flavor seems to disappear completely. Basil is at its peak in the summer and goes extremely well when paired with summer vegetables such as eggplant, peppers, zucchini, and, perhaps its best partner, tomatoes.
- **Chives**—A member of the onion family, chives have a clean, though mild, onion flavor with a slight garlic taste. Chives hold their flavor best when they are used in

dishes that are never cooked or when they are added at the very end of cooking. Because of their mild flavor, chives go best with seafood, poultry, and vegetables.

- **Cilantro**—Cilantro is one of my favorite herbs and one that I use in many recipes. The leaves and stems of the herb are known only as cilantro or Chinese parsley; the dried seed of the plant is known only as coriander. Cilantro is a staple in Mexican, Asian, and Middle Eastern cuisines. Its intoxicating, herbaceous scent and flavor go well with everything from poultry and beef to seafood and vegetables.

- **Dill**—Don't let the delicate, feathery leaves of dill fool you. This herb is packed with flavor. Used in abundance in Greek cooking, dill is a perfect match when combined with fish, chicken, yogurt, cucumbers, and potatoes.

- **Mint**—Mint's freshness should not be relegated solely to the dessert plate or iced tea. I love to use mint in savory dishes. Dried mint is pretty strong but lacks the refreshing flavor of fresh, so if you only have dried mint, use it in cooked dishes. Perfect with lamb, mint is also wonderful with fish, chicken, vegetables, vinaigrettes, and yogurt-based recipes.

- **Oregano**—There is nothing subtle about this herb with its pungent flavor and peppery kick. It is one of the few herbs that tastes almost as good dried as it does fresh. Oregano is used in abundance in Italian, Greek, and Mexican cooking and complements the flavors of pork, chicken, fish, and vegetables beautifully.

- **Parsley**—Parsley was once used only as a garnish but those days are long gone. This versatile herb is all about flavor and function. It goes virtually with everything, adding freshness to any recipe. I prefer the flat-leaf variety because it has a lot more flavor than the curly parsley, and I don't ever recommend using this herb dried.

- **Rosemary**—One of the strongest tasting of all the herbs, rosemary's piney camphor scent will add a ton of flavor to your cooking. Rosemary should be used in moderation, and its tough needlelike leaves should be finely chopped before being added to dishes. Purée sauces and vinaigrettes that feature rosemary for a smooth texture and flavor. This is another herb that holds up well when dried. Rosemary is best paired with lamb, beef, chicken, pork, and firm-fleshed fish such as tuna.

- **Sage**—My first memory of sage was the dried variety my mother used in her

Thanksgiving stuffing and the sausage patties she served with eggs on weekends. I am happy to report that sage is finally more in play in the culinary world. Like rosemary, sage needs to be used in moderation because of its strong flavor. Dried sage is even more potent than fresh, so use it sparingly. Sage has a great affinity for veal, chicken, pork, tomatoes, and white beans.

- **Tarragon**—This mild herb with a delicate anise flavor is called the "King of Herbs" by the French, and with good reason. Slightly sweet and subtly tasting of licorice, tarragon is famous for what it brings to chicken, fish, shellfish, and eggs. Dried tarragon loses its delicate flavor, becoming harsh and tasting nothing like fresh.
- **Thyme**—Another strong herb that just happens to be more versatile than rosemary and sage, thyme goes well with just about everything. I love combining it with fish, shellfish, poultry, beef, tomatoes, and—probably its most perfect companion—mushrooms.

SPICES

- **Allspice**—It may not taste like *all* spices, but you will detect cloves, cinnamon, nutmeg, and black pepper in this small berry. Allspice is the prevalent seasoning in Caribbean cooking. It enhances everything and will have everyone asking, "What is that flavor?"
- **Cinnamon**—My feeling about cinnamon is similar to my feelings about mint; it shouldn't be used just for dessert. The slightly sweet, slightly spicy flavor of cinnamon plays a big part in the seasoning of Indian and Middle Eastern dishes and adds complexity to sauces and spice rubs.
- **Coriander**—Even though this delicate and somewhat citrusy-tasting spice comes from the same plant as the herb cilantro, the flavor couldn't be more different. Coriander plays an important role in pickled foods and Indian cuisine and goes extremely well with lamb, pork, beef, and vegetables.
- **Cumin**—Pungent and smoky, cumin is the most pronounced flavoring in the majority of Mexican and Middle Eastern dishes. Lamb, chicken, fish, and avocado all benefit from the addition of this spice.

- **Paprika**—Used in abundance in Spanish and Hungarian cooking, this spice is made from a variety of dried and ground red peppers. It can be mild (sometimes called sweet) or extremely hot, so read the label before buying. I tend to use the Spanish variety, which is mild, in my cooking. For years in this country, cooks only used paprika to sprinkle on top of macaroni and cheese and deviled eggs. Today paprika's incredible flavor *and* its magnificent color are more appreciated.

- **Pepper**—Next to salt, pepper is definitely the most used seasoning in the world and the most underrated. Peppercorns come in green, white, and black varieties, and all have different flavors. I prefer the taste of black pepper in my cooking. Pepper heightens the taste of everything from meat, fish, and vegetables to even fruits such as peaches and pineapple. Whole black peppercorns hold their flavor indefinitely, so pepper should always be bought whole and ground fresh from a peppermill. You never know how long the ground pepper you find on your supermarket shelves has been sitting there, just losing flavor as the days, weeks, and even years go by.

- **Salt**—Technically a mineral, salt is not a spice and is actually classified as a seasoning or condiment. Salt, hands down, plays the most important role in cooking. Salt intensifies the taste of anything and allows the true flavors to come through. It also creates a balance between sweetness and acidity. I can't cook without a bowl of it by my side. I prefer kosher salt to standard table salt or sea salt not only for taste but also for the large fluffy grains. Its texture makes it easy to pick up with my fingers, and I always have a good feel for how much I'm using.

CHILES

I am a huge chile fan. There is a wide assortment of fresh and dried chiles available—and I make use of many of them. They all have different levels of heat as well as flavor, from peppery to fruity to earthy.

Dried Chiles and Chile Powders

Dried chiles exhibit an almost unbelievable range in the aromas and flavors they provide. Dried chiles must be softened in some way before use. This can be achieved by soaking them for 30 minutes in hot water. Of course, you can also add them directly to soups, stews, and sauces—the chiles flavor the dish and soften as they cook. To make your own chile powder, toast your chile of choice in a hot pan either over a hot grill or stove burner for about 20 seconds on each side until slightly blistered. Once cool, remove the stems and seeds, and grind in your coffee-bean-turned-spice grinder. The following are dried chiles that I use whole or powdered in my cooking.

- **Ancho chiles** are dried poblanos. I compare the flavor of these moderately hot, deep-red chiles to a spicy raisin.
- **Cascabel chiles** look like large Bing cherries. These fruity, earthy, and tealike-tasting chiles have a medium heat.
- **Chipotle chiles** are dried and smoked jalapeños with a very consistent medium to hot level of heat. They are available dried or preserved in adobo, a vinegar sauce. They are brownish in color and have an incredible fiery, smoky taste. *To make chipotle purée: Empty the entire can of chipotles preserved in adobo into a blender or food processor and process until smooth. The purée will last for months, tightly covered and stored in the refrigerator.*
- **De árbol chiles**, also called chile de árbol, are brilliant brick red with an herbal quality and a sharp, smoky flavor. Among the hottest of dried chiles, they are very spicy and are most often used in their powdered form.
- **Guajillo chiles** range in color from orange red to black brown. They have a piney, slightly fruity flavor and range in heat from mild to medium.

- **New Mexico chiles** can be used interchangeably with Anaheim chiles. Both have a deep, roasted flavor. Neither is too spicy.
- **Pasilla chiles** are also known as chiles negros, "little raisins." Named for their raisinlike aroma and shriveled, black skin, they are medium-hot and less sweet than most other dried chiles. Pasilla chiles are quite long, usually measuring 5 to 6 inches in length.

Fresh Chiles

I love the fresh, fruity, herbaceous taste that fresh chiles add to my recipes. Add them uncooked to a relish or salsa, or grill them (page 25) and purée them for use in a marinade or vinaigrette. There's no need to remove the seeds from fresh chiles; they just make the chile hotter. However you use fresh chiles, always handle them with caution, for they can severely burn your skin. Use rubber or latex gloves when preparing the chiles and be sure to keep your hands away from your eyes. Here are some of the fresh chiles that I use most often.

- **Habanero** and **Scotch bonnet** are the hottest of all chiles. These squat, lantern-shaped chiles are full of perfumed tropical flavors. Scotch bonnets are slightly smaller than habaneros. Both range in color from green to red orange, depending upon ripeness.
- **Jalapeño chiles** resemble serranos but are larger, fatter, and more tapered. When raw, jalapeños have a fresh and pure-green chile flavor. Grilling jalapeños gives them a charred, roasted flavor. Jalapeños range in flavor from medium-hot to hot and in color from green to red. Because they can vary so much in heat, it is worthwhile to taste a small piece before using. I love pickled jalapeños (page 58).
- **Poblano chiles** turn red when fully ripe but are most commonly found in their green state. They look like long, flat, dark-green bell peppers. I consider these to be the ultimate chile because of their incredible fresh pepper flavor. They are generally not too hot.
- **Serrano chiles** are among the hottest chiles available in the United States. Serranos are usually found in their green state. They become red as they ripen and

lose some of their heat. These thick-skinned chiles are slender and measure just about 2 inches long.

Chile Heat Scale

This chart rates peppers from not-hot-at-all bell peppers (0) to fiery habaneros (10). The numbering should be helpful, but keep in mind that chiles can vary in heat depending on where they are grown. If you are extremely sensitive to spicy foods, you should pretest the heat of a chile by cutting off a very small piece and tasting it raw before adding it to a recipe. Make sure to have a glass of cold milk or bowl of yogurt on hand just to be safe; dairy is the *only* way to cool the effects of a hot chile.

Chile	Heat Scale
Habanero, Scotch bonnet	10
Cayenne	8
Thai chile	7
De árbol	7
Chipotle	6
Serrano	6
Jalapeño	5
Poblano	4
Cascabel	4
Ancho	3
Guajillo	3
New Mexico	3
Pasilla	3
Bell pepper	0

Flavorings

There are so many ways to add texture, richness, and, most importantly, flavor to your food that no one should ever have to eat a bland, boring meal. I rely on an arsenal of ingredients beyond herbs and spices to make sure that my food is exciting. Here are some of the flavoring tools in my pantry and refrigerator.

CRÈME FRAÎCHE

Crème fraîche is slightly soured and thickened cream that has a smoother finish than sour cream, yet shares its tangy flavor. It is available at many supermarkets, but it is easy to make at home. Add 2 tablespoons buttermilk to 1 cup heavy cream, cover it tightly with plastic wrap, and leave it at room temperature until it thickens, from 8 to 24 hours. It will keep in your refrigerator up to 10 days. You can also substitute sour cream.

GREEK YOGURT

Incredibly thick, creamy, and less sour than standard plain yogurt, nonfat Greek yogurt tastes decadent. This is one instance when I can honestly say that I am making no concessions by using nonfat. Yogurt is great not only on its own or as the base for a sauce but also as a marinade for meats. It has remarkable tenderizing capabilities. If Greek yogurt is not available in your area, you can make a decent approximation. Put regular full-fat yogurt in a colander lined with cheesecloth or paper towels. Set the colander over a bowl to catch the liquid and put it in the refrigerator for a few hours to drain. (Starting with full-fat yogurt will raise the calorie and fat content of your finished dish, but unfortunately, standard nonfat yogurt will not achieve the right consistency.) To make about 1 cup thick yogurt, start with about $1\frac{1}{4}$ cups regular yogurt.

HONEY

This natural sweetener plays a crucial part in many of my recipes. Just a few teaspoons will balance out the strongest vinaigrette or marinade. I have kept a close eye on the amount of honey in these recipes, but I find it an indispensable flavoring. A little actually goes a long way.

VINEGARS

Vinegar is a fabulous way to add the right touch of brightness and acidity to your food. There are so many varieties out there, each with its own taste. Here are a few of my favorites:

- **Red and White Wine Vinegars** These are good all-around vinegars for salad dressings and marinades. Red is more assertive than white.
- **Sherry Vinegar** Milder and more complex than other wine vinegars, this is Spain's answer to balsamic vinegar.
- **Balsamic Vinegar** Balsamic has a concentrated, sweet, and fruity taste with exceptionally mild acidity. The more aged the balsamic vinegar is, the sweeter and thicker it becomes. Good-quality aged balsamic vinegar is very expensive and should only be used to finish a dish, such as grilled meat, fish, or vegetables. For the marinades and vinaigrettes in this book, a moderately priced balsamic from your grocery store will definitely get the job done.
- **Rice Vinegar** Made from grain, not grapes, rice vinegar is mild with a crisp, clean taste. Make sure to buy the unseasoned clear variety.
- **Cider Vinegar** Cider vinegar, made from fermented apples, is very sharp and tangy with a fruity flavor.

OILS

Oils provide richness and flavor to foods. The ones I've included in this book are also an important part of any well-balanced diet as they help maintain a healthy balance of omega-3 fatty acids.

- **Canola Oil** I use this clean, mild oil when I don't want the dish to have any taste of oil whatsoever. I use canola oil in many of my vinaigrettes, and it is the perfect oil for brushing on fruit before grilling. This is one of the most heart healthy of the vegetable oils out there.
- **Olive Oil** I use pure olive oil for cooking because of its milder taste and save the more intense extra-virgin for drizzling over finished dishes. Extra-virgin olive oil has an assertive taste that can overwhelm other flavor elements. Sometimes you just want the great taste of olive oil, but sometimes you want to make sure that everything else gets to shine, too.

GARLIC

Sharp when raw, sweet when roasted, garlic is without question the king of all flavorings! It has an oniony and, well, *garlicky* taste. It adds aroma and flavor to pretty much every dish imaginable—except, of course, desserts. I can't think of another ingredient that adds as much to whatever it touches.

ONIONS

In my opinion, everything good starts with onions and garlic. That goes for shallots, too, which taste almost like a mix between the two. Grilling onions gives them a sweet, mellow flavor that I love. Cooked and raw onions have very different qualities, each with their time and place.

CITRUS

I love the fresh taste that citrus juice and zest bring to grilled foods—especially seafood, as they highlight seafood's natural sweetness. *Orange* juice has a higher sugar content than *lemon, lime,* and *grapefruit* juices. The rind of the citrus contains no sugar at all, but it does contain the majority of the essential oil of the fruit, and that means incredible flavor. Have you ever smelled your hands after peeling an orange? That's the essential oil.

CAPERS

Capers are the unopened flower bud of a Mediterranean shrub. The buds are cured in salted white vinegar and develop a sharp, salty, sour, briny flavor. I love the salty tang capers add to my dishes. They are available packed in salt or in brine and come in different sizes. I prefer the small, brined variety, which are labeled nonpareil.

CORNICHONS

Cornichons are tiny French pickled gherkins. They are super sour and maintain a great crunch when chopped and added to salads. Previously available only in specialty shops, they can now be found in most supermarkets.

TAHINI

Tahini is a spread made from sesame seeds—the sesame equivalent of natural peanut butter. It has a strong, nutty flavor that adds great depth to sauces, vinaigrettes, and, of course, classic hummus.

How to . . .

ROAST PEPPERS AND CHILES ON THE GRILL

Heat your grill to high. Brush the peppers with olive oil, season with salt and pepper, and grill until charred on all sides, 8 to 10 minutes. Place the grilled peppers in a bowl, cover with plastic wrap, and let sit for 15 minutes. Then peel, halve, stem, and seed them. Chop or slice as desired. Treat fresh chiles exactly the same way.

ROAST GARLIC ON THE GRILL OR IN THE OVEN

Grill

Heat your grill to medium. Separate the cloves of a head of garlic (do not peel). Drizzle the cloves with olive oil and season with salt and pepper. Wrap the garlic securely in aluminum foil and place on the grate of the grill. Close the cover and grill for 45 minutes to 1 hour until very soft. Squeeze the pulp from the skins, discarding the skins.

Oven

Preheat the oven to 325 degrees F. Proceed as above but roast on the middle rack of the oven instead of on the grill.

GRILL ONIONS

Peel the onions and cut them crosswise into 1/4-inch-thick slices. Brush the slices with oil and lightly season with salt and pepper. Grill the slices for 3 to 4 minutes per side over high heat until slightly charred and just cooked through.

GRILL CITRUS

Cut oranges, lemons, limes, or grapefruits in half crosswise. Brush the cut sides lightly with canola oil and place cut side down on the grill. Grill until golden brown, 2 to 3 minutes. Cut each piece in half again or cut bigger fruits into quarters. Serve hot.

SEGMENT CITRUS FRUIT

Use a sharp knife to slice off the top and bottom of the citrus fruit, removing a little of the flesh of each end too. Stand the fruit on one end and position your knife just to the inside of the citrus rind, where the flesh meets the bitter-tasting white pith. Following the curve of the fruit, slice off as much pith as possible; you'll need to remove a sliver of flesh to do this. Once all of the rind and pith are removed, hold the fruit in one hand and carefully cut into the fruit along both sides of each membrane to release the citrus sections. When all of the sections are free, squeeze the empty membranes in your hand over a bowl to capture any remaining juice. You can cover and refrigerate the sections and their juice for up to 1 day.

TOAST NUTS, SEEDS, AND SPICES ON THE GRILL

Heat your grill to medium-low. Put a single layer of nuts or seeds in a skillet or sauté pan and heat for 5 to 7 minutes until light golden brown and fragrant, shaking the pan every couple of minutes to prevent burning. For spices, proceed as above but reduce the cooking time to 3 to 4 minutes, until the spices are just fragrant. Transfer the nuts, seeds, or spices to a plate and let cool completely.

BLANCH VEGETABLES

Blanching is used to partially cook food, most often vegetables. This technique retains the bright color of the vegetable and tenderizes it slightly. Salting the water helps green vegetables stay green and also brings out their flavor. Bring a large pot of salted water to a boil over high heat. While the water is coming to a boil, fill a medium bowl halfway with ice and add enough water to come just to the top of the ice. Add the vegetables to the pot and boil for 2 minutes. Use a slotted spoon to remove the vegetables to the ice water; let sit for 1 minute until cool. Drain well.

VEGETABLES

Grilled Asparagus and Egg Salad with Tarragon-Caper Vinaigrette

This nutritious salad is really enhanced by the anise-flavored tarragon vinaigrette. I would serve this springtime salad year-round alongside the yogurt-marinated leg of lamb (page 178).

Serves 6

1½ pounds medium asparagus,
    trimmed
½ cup plus 1 tablespoon olive oil
Freshly ground black pepper
4 hard-cooked eggs (page 118),
    whites and yolks separated,
    whites finely chopped
¼ cup white wine vinegar
¼ cup cold water
1 tablespoon finely chopped fresh
    tarragon leaves
2 tablespoons capers, drained
6 cornichons, finely chopped

Nutritional Analysis (per serving)

Calories: **300**   Protein (gm): **7**   Carbohydrates (gm): **16**

Total Sugar (gm): **4**   Total Fat (gm): **24**   Saturated Fat (gm): **4**

Cholesterol (mg): **141**   Sodium (mg): **458**   Fiber (gm): **3**

1. Heat your grill to high.

2. Brush the asparagus with 1 tablespoon of the oil and season with pepper. Lay the asparagus crosswise on the grate and grill until just cooked through, 3 minutes per side. Remove from the grill and place on a platter.

3. Combine the cooked egg yolks, vinegar, water, tarragon, and ¼ teaspoon pepper in a blender and blend until smooth. With the motor running, slowly add the remaining ½ cup oil and blend until emulsified. Scrape the mixture into a bowl and stir in the capers and cornichons.

4. Spoon the vinaigrette over the asparagus, then sprinkle with the chopped egg whites.

Grilled Antipasto
with Gorgonzola Vinaigrette

Use your creativity when arranging this antipasto platter filled with beautiful, nutritious vegetables. Serve this dish family style in order to show it off to its fullest potential.

Serves 6

2 red bell peppers

2 yellow bell peppers

12 ounces medium asparagus, trimmed

2 Japanese eggplants, halved lengthwise

2 small yellow squash, halved lengthwise

2 large portobello mushrooms, stemmed

¾ cup olive oil

2 teaspoons kosher salt

2 teaspoons freshly ground black pepper

½ cup pitted assorted olives

¼ cup balsamic vinegar

1 teaspoon chopped fresh thyme leaves

4 ounces Gorgonzola cheese, crumbled

Nutritional Analysis (per serving)

Calories: **383**   Protein (gm): **9**   Carbohydrates (gm): **24**

Total Sugar (gm): **11**   Total Fat (gm): **30**   Saturated Fat (gm): **7**

Cholesterol (mg): **17**   Sodium (mg): **410**   Fiber (gm): **10**

1. Heat your grill to high. Brush the vegetables and mushrooms with ¼ cup of the oil and season with 1¾ teaspoons of the salt and 1¾ teaspoons of the pepper.

2. Grill the peppers, turning as needed, until charred on all sides, 8 to 10 minutes. Remove from the grill, place in a paper bag or a bowl covered with plastic wrap, and let sit for 15 minutes. Remove and discard the skins, stems, and seeds, then cut the flesh into eighths.

3. Lay the asparagus crosswise on the grate and turn as needed until just cooked through, 3 minutes per side.

4. Grill the eggplants and squash cut side down for 3 minutes. Turn them over and continue grilling until just cooked through, 4 to 5 minutes longer. Remove from the grill and cut crosswise into ½-inch-thick slices.

5. Grill the mushrooms for 4 to 5 minutes per side until just cooked through. Remove from the grill and cut into ¼-inch-thick slices.

6. Arrange the vegetables on a large platter and scatter the olives around the platter.

7. Whisk together the vinegar, thyme, and remaining ¼ teaspoon salt and ¼ teaspoon pepper in a medium bowl. Slowly drizzle in the remaining ½ cup olive oil, whisking until emulsified. Stir in the Gorgonzola.

8. Drizzle the vinaigrette over the vegetables; serve warm or at room temperature.

Grilled and Marinated Zucchini and Yellow Squash

It's amazing how a quick and simple marinade can change the flavor of zucchini and yellow squash. This lemony-peppery mixture really wakes them up. This may seem to be in reverse order—grill, then marinate—but it's a classic Italian technique that creates great results.

Serves 4

2 medium zucchini, halved lengthwise

2 medium yellow squash, halved lengthwise

¼ cup plus 1 tablespoon olive oil

½ teaspoon kosher salt

½ teaspoon freshly ground black pepper

2 tablespoons fresh lemon juice

2 teaspoons grated lemon zest

Pinch of red pepper flakes

2 tablespoons finely chopped fresh basil leaves

1. Heat your grill to high.

2. Brush the zucchini and yellow squash with 1 tablespoon of the oil and season with ¼ teaspoon of the salt and ¼ teaspoon of the pepper. Grill cut side down until light

---

Nutritional Analysis (per serving)

Calories: **181**   Protein (gm): **2**   Carbohydrates (gm): **7**

Total Sugar (gm): **2**   Total Fat (gm): **17**   Saturated Fat (gm): **2**

Cholesterol (mg): **0**   Sodium (mg): **152**   Fiber (gm): **3**

golden brown, 3 to 4 minutes. Turn them over and continue grilling until just cooked through, 4 to 5 minutes longer. Remove from the grill and cut crosswise into $\frac{1}{2}$-inch-thick slices.

3. Whisk together the remaining $\frac{1}{4}$ cup oil, the lemon juice, zest, red pepper flakes, and the remaining $\frac{1}{4}$ teaspoon salt and $\frac{1}{4}$ teaspoon pepper in a large bowl. Add the zucchini, squash, and basil and toss to coat. Cover and let sit at room temperature for at least 30 minutes and up to 2 hours before serving.

Grilled Asian-Style Eggplant Salad

Whenever I go to an Asian restaurant, whether it is Chinese, Japanese, or Thai, I always order the eggplant. Asian flavors have a great affinity for eggplant. Here is my take, hot off the grill!

Serves 4

---

8 cloves garlic, roasted (page 25)

¼ cup rice vinegar

1 tablespoon low-sodium soy sauce

1 tablespoon water

¼ teaspoon red pepper flakes

¼ cup plus 2 tablespoons canola oil

4 Japanese eggplants, halved lengthwise

1 teaspoon kosher salt

1 teaspoon freshly ground black pepper

12 fresh basil leaves, cut into thin ribbons

---

1. Combine the garlic, vinegar, soy sauce, water, and pepper flakes in a blender and blend until smooth. With the motor running, slowly add ¼ cup of the oil and blend until emulsified.

2. Heat your grill to medium.

Nutritional Analysis (per serving)

Calories: **174**   Protein (gm): **2**   Carbohydrates (gm): **11**

Total Sugar (gm): **3.8**   Total Fat (gm): **14**   Saturated Fat (gm): **1**

Cholesterol (mg): **0**   Sodium (mg): **155**   Fiber (gm): **5**

3. Brush the eggplants with the remaining 2 tablespoons oil and season with the salt and pepper. Place the eggplants cut side down on the grill and cook until slightly charred, 4 to 5 minutes. Turn the eggplants over, close the hood of the grill, and cook until just cooked through, 4 to 5 minutes longer. Remove from the grill and cut into ½-inch pieces.

4. Transfer the eggplants to a medium bowl, add the vinaigrette and basil, and toss gently to combine. Cover and let sit at room temperature for at least 30 minutes and up to 2 hours before serving.

Grilled Zucchini Succotash

Originally a Native American preparation, this now classic Southern dish moved again—this time to the grill. The creamy texture of *queso fresco,* a Mexican fresh cheese, not only adds richness to the recipe but also slightly tempers the heat of the chiles. If *queso fresco* is not available in your area, farmer's cheese would be a perfect substitute.

Serves 6

3 medium zucchini, halved lengthwise

2 tablespoons olive oil

½ teaspoon kosher salt

1 teaspoon freshly ground black pepper

1 medium red onion, finely chopped

2 cloves garlic, finely chopped

1 cup fresh lima beans, blanched (pages 26–27),
    or frozen lima beans, thawed

Kernels from 2 ears of fresh corn

1 cup low-sodium vegetable stock

1 plum tomato, halved, seeded, and chopped

1 poblano chile, grilled (page 25), peeled,
    seeded, and chopped

1 jalapeño, grilled (page 25), peeled, seeded,
    and chopped

Nutritional Analysis (per serving)

Calories: **159**   Protein (gm): **8**   Carbohydrates (gm): **24**

Total Sugar (gm): **5.5**   Total Fat (gm): **5**   Saturated Fat (gm): **1.4**

Cholesterol (mg): **7**   Sodium (mg): **141**   Fiber (gm): **5**

½ **cup crumbled** *queso fresco*
or fresh farmer's cheese
¼ **cup chopped fresh cilantro leaves**

1. Heat your grill to high.

2. Brush the cut sides of the zucchini with 1 tablespoon of the oil and season with ¼ teaspoon of the salt and ¼ teaspoon of the pepper. Grill cut side down until light golden brown, 3 to 4 minutes. Turn them over and continue grilling until just cooked through, 4 to 5 minutes longer. Remove from the grill and cut into small dice.

3. Heat the remaining 1 tablespoon oil in a medium saucepan on the grate of the grill. Add the onion and cook, stirring, until soft, 3 to 4 minutes. Add the garlic and cook for 1 minute. Add the lima beans, corn, and stock and simmer for 5 minutes. Add the tomato, chiles, grilled zucchini, and remaining ¼ teaspoon salt and ¾ teaspoon pepper. Cook for 2 minutes.

4. Remove from the grill and stir in the cheese and cilantro. Serve warm or at room temperature.

Grilled Fennel and Orange Salad
with Almonds and Mint

This crunchy salad is a Sicilian classic. Fennel and mint (so great together) are often paired in Italian cooking—as are oranges and almonds.

Serves 4

2 bulbs fennel, trimmed, halved, and cut
    into ½-inch-thick slices
¼ cup plus 2 tablespoons olive oil
1 teaspoon kosher salt
½ teaspoon freshly ground black pepper
2 oranges, segmented (page 26)
2 tablespoons fresh orange juice
1 teaspoon grated orange zest
¼ cup sliced almonds, toasted (page 26)
2 tablespoons chopped fresh mint leaves

1. Heat your grill to high.

2. Brush the fennel with 2 tablespoons of the olive oil and season with ¾ teaspoon of the salt and ¼ teaspoon of the pepper. Grill for 3 to 4 minutes per side until slightly charred

Nutritional Analysis (per serving)

Calories: **274**   Protein (gm): **3**   Carbohydrates (gm): **15**

Total Sugar (gm): **3**   Total Fat (gm): **24**   Saturated Fat (gm): **3**

Cholesterol (mg): **0**   Sodium (mg): **341**   Fiber (gm): **5**

and almost cooked through. Place the fennel on a platter and scatter the orange segments over the top.

3. Whisk together the orange juice, zest, remaining ¼ cup olive oil, and remaining ¼ teaspoon salt and ¼ teaspoon pepper. Drizzle over the salad, then sprinkle with the almonds and mint. Serve immediately or at room temperature.

Grilled German Sweet Potato Salad

My grandmother never made her potato salad with sweet potatoes, and she sure didn't grill them, but this dish reminds me of my childhood anyway. The flavors of the family staple are still there—smoky bacon, sharp Dijon mustard, and slightly sweet, slightly tangy cider vinegar.

Serves 6

3 large sweet potatoes (do not peel)
4 ounces (8 slices) bacon, finely diced
1 small yellow onion, halved and thinly sliced
½ cup cider vinegar
1 tablespoon Dijon mustard
¼ cup plus 3 tablespoons canola oil
1 tablespoon chopped fresh thyme leaves
1¼ teaspoons freshly ground black pepper
1 teaspoon kosher salt

1. In a large pot of salted water, boil the potatoes until just cooked through but not completely soft, 20 to 30 minutes depending on size. Test by piercing a potato with a thin bamboo skewer; when the skewer meets some resistance but can slide all the way through, the potatoes are ready. Drain the potatoes immediately and set aside until cool enough to handle.

Nutritional Analysis (per serving)

Calories: **374**	Protein (gm): **9**	Carbohydrates (gm): **27**
Total Sugar (gm): **3**	Total Fat (gm): **26**	Saturated Fat (gm): **4**
Cholesterol (mg): **20**	Sodium (mg): **694**	Fiber (gm): **3**

2. Heat your grill to high.

3. Cook the bacon in a medium sauté pan over medium heat until golden brown and slightly crunchy, 4 to 5 minutes. Remove the bacon with a slotted spoon to a plate lined with paper towels.

4. Return the pan to the heat and add the onion to the rendered bacon fat. Cook, stirring occasionally, over medium heat until soft, 4 to 5 minutes. Add the vinegar and cook for 1 minute. Remove from the heat and whisk in the mustard, ¼ cup of the oil, the thyme, and ¼ teaspoon of the pepper. Cover and keep warm on a cooler part of the grill while you grill the potatoes.

5. Cut the potatoes into ¼-inch-thick slices. Brush both sides of the potato slices with the remaining 3 tablespoons oil and season with the salt and remaining 1 teaspoon pepper. Grill until lightly browned on both sides and just cooked through, about 5 minutes total.

6. Place the potatoes in a bowl and toss while still warm with the dressing. Sprinkle with the bacon. Serve warm or at room temperature.

Grilled Sweet Potato Salad with Pancetta and Rosemary Vinaigrette

The natural sweetness of the potatoes is a perfect base for this Italian-inspired salad. Be sure to add the dressing to the sweet potatoes while they are still warm, so they soak up the maximum amount of flavor.

Serves 6

3 large sweet potatoes (do not peel)
¼ cup plus 3 tablespoons olive oil
4 ounces pancetta, finely diced
1 medium shallot, thinly sliced
¼ cup red wine vinegar
2 teaspoons finely chopped fresh rosemary leaves
1½ teaspoons freshly ground black pepper
1 teaspoon kosher salt

1. In a large pot of salted water, boil the potatoes until just cooked through but not completely soft, 20 to 30 minutes depending on size. Test by piercing a potato with a thin bamboo skewer; when the skewer meets some resistance but can slide all the way through, the potatoes are ready. Drain the potatoes immediately and set aside until cool enough to handle.

Nutritional Analysis (per serving)

Calories: **285**	Protein (gm): **5**	Carbohydrates (gm): **27**
Total Sugar (gm): **6**	Total Fat (gm): **18**	Saturated Fat (gm): **2**
Cholesterol (mg): **7**	Sodium (mg): **276**	Fiber (gm): **5**

2. Heat your grill to high.

3. Heat 1 tablespoon of the olive oil in a medium sauté pan over high heat. Add the pancetta and cook until golden brown and crisp, 4 to 5 minutes. Remove the pancetta from the pan with a slotted spoon to a plate lined with paper towels.

4. Return the pan to the heat and add the shallot to the rendered fat. Cook until golden brown and slightly caramelized, 2 to 3 minutes. Add the vinegar and cook for 1 minute. Remove the pan from the heat and whisk in ¼ cup olive oil, the rosemary, and ½ teaspoon of the pepper. Cover and keep warm on a cooler part of the grill while you cook the potatoes.

5. Cut the potatoes into ¼-inch-thick slices. Brush both sides of the potato slices with the remaining 2 tablespoons oil and season with the salt and remaining 1 teaspoon pepper. Grill until lightly browned on both sides and just cooked through, about 5 minutes total.

6. Place the potatoes in a bowl and toss while still warm with the dressing. Sprinkle with the pancetta. Serve warm or at room temperature.

Grilled Portobello Mushrooms Stacked with Spinach and Manchego Cheese

When grilled, portobello mushrooms take on an incredibly satisfying meaty quality. I think of this dish as a first-course salad, but it could easily be the centerpiece of a vegetarian meal. Stack the mushrooms for that professional chef look and be sure to shave the cheese with a vegetable peeler.

Serves 4

SHERRY VINAIGRETTE

1 small shallot, finely chopped
¼ cup sherry vinegar or balsamic vinegar
2 teaspoons Dijon mustard
¼ teaspoon kosher salt
¼ teaspoon freshly ground black pepper
¼ cup olive oil

Whisk together the shallot, vinegar, mustard, salt, and pepper in a small bowl. Slowly drizzle in the oil and whisk until emulsified.

Nutritional Analysis (per serving)

Calories: **210**	Protein (gm): **10**	Carbohydrates (gm): **12.5**
Total Sugar (gm): **4**	Total Fat (gm): **15**	Saturated Fat (gm): **4**
Cholesterol (mg): **10**	Sodium (mg): **600**	Fiber (gm): **8**

GRILLED MUSHROOMS

8 medium portobello mushroom caps

2 tablespoons olive oil

1 teaspoon kosher salt

1 teaspoon freshly ground black pepper

8 ounces baby spinach

**2 ounces Manchego cheese, thinly shaved
with a vegetable peeler**

2 tablespoons finely chopped fresh chives

1. Heat your grill to high.

2. Brush the mushroom caps on both sides with the oil and season with the salt and pepper. Grill top side down until slightly charred, 3 to 4 minutes. Turn the mushrooms over and continue to grill until just cooked through, 3 to 4 minutes longer.

3. Place the spinach in a medium bowl and toss with some of the sherry vinaigrette. Divide half of the spinach among 4 salad plates. Top with half of the Manchego and then a mushroom. Repeat the layers in the same order using the remaining spinach and cheese, and ending with a mushroom cap. Press down gently on the stacks to keep them from falling.

4. Drizzle the remaining vinaigrette over the mushrooms and garnish with the chives. Serve immediately.

Red Cabbage and Beet Slaw

Everyone has their own version of cole slaw, and I haven't tasted one that isn't great with grilled foods. This ruby-red slaw flecked with bright green cilantro is no exception, and it's also a delicious way to add color to your table. The raw beets are a delightful surprise—sweet and crunchy. Cooking the onions softens their bite, but the horseradish keeps the slaw sharp.

Serves 6

¼ cup plus 1 tablespoon olive oil

¼ cup sherry vinegar or balsamic vinegar

2 tablespoons prepared horseradish, drained

¼ teaspoon kosher salt

¼ teaspoon freshly ground black pepper

1 medium red onion, halved and thinly sliced

1 medium head red cabbage, thinly sliced

1 large red beet, peeled and coarsely grated

¼ cup coarsely chopped fresh cilantro leaves

Nutritional Analysis (per serving)

Calories: **127**   Protein (gm): **1**   Carbohydrates (gm): **6**

Total Sugar (gm): **4**   Total Fat (gm): **11**   Saturated Fat (gm): **1.5**

Cholesterol (mg): **0**   Sodium (mg): **79**   Fiber (gm): **1**

1. Whisk together ¼ cup of the oil, the vinegar, horseradish, salt, and pepper in a large bowl.

2. Heat the remaining 1 tablespoon oil in a large sauté pan over medium-high heat. Add the onion and cook, stirring occasionally, until soft, 3 to 4 minutes. Add the cabbage, cover and cook until just wilted but slightly crunchy, 5 to 6 minutes. Transfer the cabbage mixture to the bowl with the vinaigrette, add the beet and cilantro, and toss well to combine. Cover and let sit at room temperature for at least 30 minutes and up to 2 hours before serving.

Bulgur Salad with Green Onion Vinaigrette

This is my take on tabbouleh, the classic Middle Eastern salad that is incredibly flavorful and healthy and a perfect accompaniment to grilled meat and fish. The green onion, which is usually served as part of the salad, now plays a starring role in the vinaigrette.

Serves 6

4¼ cups water

3 teaspoons kosher salt

¾ cup medium-grind bulgur

1 small red onion, finely chopped

2 plum tomatoes, finely chopped

1 cup finely chopped fresh flat-leaf
   parsley leaves

½ cup finely chopped fresh mint leaves

¼ cup fresh lime juice

1 teaspoon honey

½ cup chopped green onions (approximately 6)

1 serrano chile, chopped

½ teaspoon freshly ground black pepper

½ cup olive oil

Nutritional Analysis (per serving)

Calories: **241**   Protein (gm): **3**   Carbohydrates (gm): **18**

Total Sugar (gm): **2.6**   Total Fat (gm): **18**   Saturated Fat (gm): **2.4**

Cholesterol (mg): **0**   Sodium (mg): **198**   Fiber (gm): **4.4**

1. Combine 4 cups of the water with 2 teaspoons of the salt in a medium saucepan and bring to a boil. Place the bulgur in a large bowl, pour the boiling water over, cover the bowl with plastic wrap, and let sit until the bulgur is tender, 10 to 15 minutes.

2. Drain the bulgur in a sieve and press on the bulgur with your hand to squeeze out as much water as possible. Return the bulgur to the bowl and mix in the onion, tomatoes, parsley, and mint. Transfer the bulgur salad to a platter.

3. Combine the lime juice, remaining ¼ cup water, the honey, green onions, chile, remaining teaspoon salt, and pepper in a blender and blend until smooth. With the motor running, slowly drizzle in the olive oil and blend until emulsified.

4. Drizzle the vinaigrette over the bulgur salad and gently toss to combine. Serve warm or at room temperature.

Grilled Spice-Rubbed Vidalia Onions

These tasty onion rings never hit the deep fryer—they get their flavor and crust from the spice mix and a turn on the grill. I like these guys even better than the old beer-battered ones.

Serves 6

2 tablespoons paprika

1 tablespoon ancho chile powder

2 teaspoons ground cumin

2 teaspoons ground coriander

2 teaspoons kosher salt

1 teaspoon freshly ground black
    pepper

1 teaspoon cayenne

1 teaspoon dry mustard

1 teaspoon dried oregano

4 Vidalia onions, cut into
    ¼-inch-thick slices

¼ cup canola oil

Nutritional Analysis (per serving)

Calories: **141**   Protein (gm): **2**   Carbohydrates (gm): **14**

Total Sugar (gm): **0**   Total Fat (gm): **10**   Saturated Fat (gm): **1**

Cholesterol (mg): **0**   Sodium (mg): **392**   Fiber (gm): **4**

1. Heat your grill to medium-high. Whisk together all of the seasonings in a small bowl.

2. Brush the onion slices on both sides with the oil. Rub one side of each onion slice with the seasoning mixture and place rub side down on the grill. Grill until golden brown and a crust has formed, 2 to 3 minutes. Turn the onions over and continue grilling until just cooked through, 2 to 3 minutes longer. Serve hot or at room temperature.

Twice-Grilled Peppers with Buffalo Mozzarella and Caper-Basil Vinaigrette

Italy on the grill. Grilling the peppers twice enables the smoky flavor of the grill to fully permeate the peppers' flesh. They pair superbly with creamy mozzarella.

Serves 6

CAPER-BASIL VINAIGRETTE

3 tablespoons red wine vinegar

1 teaspoon Dijon mustard

1 clove garlic, finely chopped

¼ teaspoon kosher salt

¼ teaspoon freshly ground
 black pepper

¼ cup olive oil

2 tablespoons capers, drained

2 tablespoons chopped fresh
 basil leaves

Whisk together the vinegar, mustard, garlic, salt, and pepper in a medium bowl. Slowly drizzle in the oil and whisk until emulsified. Stir in the capers and basil.

Nutritional Analysis (per serving)

Calories: **385**   Protein (gm): **15**   Carbohydrates (gm): **11**

Total Sugar (gm): **4.7**   Total Fat (gm): **27**   Saturated Fat (gm): **9.5**

Cholesterol (mg): **27**   Sodium (mg): **126**   Fiber (gm): **2**

TWICE-GRILLED PEPPERS

3 red bell peppers
3 yellow bell peppers
3 orange bell peppers
3 tablespoons olive oil
¾ teaspoon kosher salt
¾ teaspoon freshly ground black pepper
1 pound buffalo mozzarella, cut into ¼-inch-thick slices
Fresh basil leaves

1. Heat your grill to high.

2. Brush the peppers with 2 tablespoons of the oil and season with ½ teaspoon of the salt and ½ teaspoon of the pepper. Grill the peppers until charred on all sides, 8 to 10 minutes. Remove from the grill, place in a bowl, cover with plastic wrap, and let sit for 15 minutes.

3. Remove the skins, stems, and seeds from the peppers and cut the flesh into 1-inch-thick strips. Brush the peppers with the remaining 1 tablespoon oil and season with the remaining ¼ teaspoon salt and ¼ teaspoon pepper.

4. Return the peppers to the grill, laying them crosswise on the grate, and cook until slightly charred on both sides, 2 minutes per side.

5. Arrange the peppers and mozzarella on a platter and drizzle with the caper-basil vinaigrette. Garnish with basil leaves. Serve at room temperature.

Grilled New Potatoes
with Lemon-Garlic Aïoli and Chives

The lemony flavor of this aïoli really pops on grilled new potatoes. When shopping for your produce, look for the smallest potatoes you can find. The smaller they are, the more tender they will be.

Serves 6

3 pounds small new potatoes (do not peel)

¾ cup mayonnaise

6 cloves garlic, coarsely chopped

¼ cup fresh lemon juice

2 teaspoons grated lemon zest

½ teaspoon kosher salt

½ teaspoon freshly ground black pepper

3 tablespoons olive oil

¼ cup finely chopped fresh chives

1. In a large pot of salted water, boil the potatoes until just cooked through but not completely soft, 10 to 15 minutes depending on size. Test by piercing a potato with a thin bamboo skewer; when the skewer meets some resistance but can slide all the way

Nutritional Analysis (per serving)

Calories: **426** Protein (gm): **4** Carbohydrates (gm): **37**

Total Sugar (gm): **3** Total Fat (gm): **29** Saturated Fat (gm): **4**

Cholesterol (mg): **10** Sodium (mg): **222** Fiber (gm): **6**

through, the potatoes are ready. Drain the potatoes immediately and set aside until cool enough to handle.

2. Combine the mayonnaise, garlic, lemon juice, zest, ¼ teaspoon of the salt, and ¼ teaspoon of the pepper in a blender and blend until smooth.

3. Heat your grill to high.

4. Cut the potatoes in half, brush the cut sides with the oil, and season with the remaining ¼ teaspoon salt and ¼ teaspoon pepper. Grill the potatoes cut side down until golden brown and just cooked through, 2 to 3 minutes.

5. Place the potatoes on a platter, drizzle with the aïoli, and sprinkle with the chives. Serve warm.

Pickled Jalapeños

This is a great way to add POW to your dishes without adding fat or calories. They are great on burgers, hot dogs, sausages, and, of course, nachos. The fresh flavor and texture of these pickled jalapeños kicks the old canned version to the curb.

Makes 10 to 15 pickled jalapeños

3 cups white wine vinegar

1 cup red wine vinegar

3 tablespoons sugar

1 teaspoon black peppercorns

1 teaspoon coriander seeds

1 teaspoon fennel seeds

1 teaspoon mustard seeds

½ teaspoon cumin seeds

2 tablespoons kosher salt

3 tablespoons fresh cilantro leaves

10 to 15 jalapeños (depending on their size)

1. Combine all of the ingredients except for the cilantro and jalapeños in a medium saucepan and bring to a boil. Boil for 2 minutes, remove from the heat and let sit for 5 minutes before adding the cilantro.

Nutritional Analysis (per jalapeño)

Calories: **12**   Protein (gm): **0**   Carbohydrates (gm): **2**

Total Sugar (gm): **1**   Total Fat (gm): **0**   Saturated Fat (gm): **0**

Cholesterol (mg): **0**   Sodium (mg): **87**   Fiber (gm): **.5**

2. Pack the jalapeños into a quart-size Mason jar or place in a medium bowl. Pour the warm vinegar mixture over them, cover and refrigerate for at least 24 hours and up to 2 weeks.

FISH AND SHELLFISH

Buckwheat Pizza with Cilantro Pesto, Jack Cheese, and Grilled Shrimp

Buckwheat is loaded with nutrients, including protein, and has a nutty, earthy flavor that provides the perfect base for grilled pizza. Pumpkin seeds and cilantro replace the traditional Italian pine nuts and basil in this Southwestern pesto. Plump shrimp and melted Monterey Jack cheese are the perfect accompaniments. Pizza on the grill can seem intimidating but, trust me, you'll be amazed at how easy it is.

Serves 6

BUCKWHEAT FLATBREAD

1¼ cups warm (105 to 115 degrees F) water

1 teaspoon dried yeast

Pinch of sugar

1¼ to 1¾ cups all-purpose flour, plus more for rolling

¾ cup buckwheat flour

1 teaspoon salt

2 tablespoons olive oil

---

1. In the bowl of an electric mixer fitted with the paddle attachment, combine the water, yeast, and sugar. Mix for 1 minute on low speed, then let sit until the mixture just begins to bubble, about 5 minutes. Attach the dough hook and add 1¼ cups of the flour, the buckwheat flour, and salt to the yeast mixture. Mix on high speed until the dough forms

---

Nutritional Analysis (per serving with 2 tablespoons pesto)

Calories: **451**	Protein (gm): **15**	Carbohydrates (gm): **32**
Total Sugar (gm): **1**	Total Fat (gm): **30**	Saturated Fat (gm): **7**
Cholesterol (mg): **47**	Sodium (mg): **820**	Fiber (gm): **3**

a mass, 2 to 3 minutes; the dough should be sticky. Add up to $\frac{1}{2}$ cup additional flour if necessary for a dough dry enough to roll out.

2. Divide the dough into quarters, roll into balls, and lightly brush with the oil. Place on a floured surface and cover the balls loosely with plastic wrap and a clean cloth. Let rise for 2 hours at room temperature, or place on a lightly greased baking sheet or in 4 medium bowls, cover, and let rise overnight in the refrigerator.

CILANTRO PESTO
$\frac{3}{4}$ cup fresh cilantro leaves
$\frac{1}{4}$ cup fresh flat-leaf parsley leaves
2 cloves garlic, coarsely chopped
3 tablespoons pumpkin seeds
$\frac{1}{2}$ cup olive oil
$\frac{1}{4}$ cup grated Parmesan cheese
$\frac{1}{4}$ teaspoon kosher salt
$\frac{1}{4}$ teaspoon freshly ground black pepper

Combine the cilantro, parsley, garlic, and pumpkin seeds in a food processor or blender and process until coarsely chopped. With the motor running, slowly add the oil and process until the mixture is smooth. Add the cheese, salt, and pepper and process for a few seconds longer until combined. If the mixture appears too pasty, add a few tablespoons of water to thin it slightly. *The pesto can be made up to 1 day in advance, covered, and kept refrigerated.*

GRILLED SHRIMP
3 tablespoons olive oil
$1\frac{1}{2}$ teaspoons kosher salt
$1\frac{1}{2}$ teaspoons freshly ground black pepper
16 large shrimp, peeled and deveined
4 ounces shredded Monterey Jack cheese
Chopped fresh cilantro leaves

1. Heat your grill to high.

2. To form the flatbreads, pat each piece of dough out on a lightly floured surface and sprinkle liberally with flour. Roll each disk into an 8-inch circle. Prick the dough liberally with a fork to keep it from rising. Brush both sides of the dough with 2 tablespoons of the oil and season with 1 teaspoon of the salt and 1 teaspoon of the pepper.

3. Grill the flatbreads until they are golden brown on each side, about 2 minutes per side. Remove from the grill and set aside for the moment.

4. Brush the shrimp with the remaining 1 tablespoon oil and season with the remaining ½ teaspoon salt and ½ teaspoon pepper. Grill for 1 to 2 minutes per side until slightly charred and just cooked through. Transfer the shrimp to a plate.

5. Spread 2 tablespoons of the pesto over each flatbread and divide the cheese on top of the pesto. Arrange the shrimp on top of the cheese and place the flatbreads back on the grill. Close the cover of the grill or cover the flatbreads loosely with foil and cook until the cheese has melted and the dough is cooked through, 2 to 3 minutes. Remove from the grill and garnish with fresh cilantro before serving.

SHRIMP SIZES

My recipes call for shrimp of a certain size, usually medium and large. Shrimp is graded according to the number of the shellfish it takes to make a pound. The larger the number, the smaller the shrimp.

Extra-Colossal = Less than 10 per pound

Colossal = Less than 15 per pound

Extra-Jumbo = 16 to 20 per pound

Jumbo = 21 to 25 per pound

Extra-Large = 26 to 30 per pound

Large = 31 to 40 per pound

Medium-Large = 36 to 40 per pound

Medium = 41 to 50 per pound

Small = 51 to 60 per pound

Extra-Small = 61 to 70 per pound

Tiny = Over 70 per pound

Garlic–Red Chile–Thyme–Marinated Shrimp

Reading the ingredient list could scare you off, but don't worry, the chiles I call for aren't too spicy. These shrimp are earthy and garlicky, not burn-your-mouth hot. Don't marinate the shrimp for longer than 15 minutes. Left too long in any marinade, shrimp and other seafood begin to break down.

Serves 6

2 ancho chiles
1 New Mexico chile
1 pasilla chile
½ cup canola oil
8 cloves garlic, coarsely chopped
3 tablespoons chopped fresh
    thyme leaves
1 teaspoon salt
1 teaspoon freshly ground
    black pepper
2 pounds large shrimp in the shell

1. Place all of the chiles in a large bowl, cover with boiling water, and let sit for at least 30 minutes to soften.

Nutritional Analysis (per serving)

Calories: **274**   Protein (gm): **32**   Carbohydrates (gm): **8**

Total Sugar (gm): **0**   Total Fat (gm): **12**   Saturated Fat (gm): **1**

Cholesterol (mg): **230**   Sodium (mg): **415**   Fiber (gm): **2**

2. Remove the chiles from the water. Stem, seed, and coarsely chop them and place in a blender with ¼ cup of the soaking liquid. Add the oil, garlic, thyme, ½ teaspoon of the salt, and ½ teaspoon of the pepper and blend until smooth.

3. Place the shrimp in a large bowl, pour the chile marinade over, and let marinate for 15 minutes at room temperature.

4. Heat your grill to high.

5. Remove the shrimp from the marinade, season with the remaining ½ teaspoon salt and ½ teaspoon pepper, and grill for 1½ to 2 minutes per side until just cooked through. Serve immediately. Peel and discard the shells before eating.

Grilled Prawns with Spicy Fresh Pepper Sauce

This electric sauce fires up the prawns with a combination of serrano and poblano chiles and red pepper flakes. The yellow bell pepper's sweetness keeps the heat in check. Leaving the heads on the prawns not only makes for a dramatic presentation but also helps stop the prawns from drying out on the grill. But don't worry if you can't find them with their heads—headless is fine.

Serves 4

FRESH PEPPER SAUCE

1¼ cups olive oil

1 yellow bell pepper, grilled (page 25),
    peeled, seeded, and finely diced

1 serrano chile, grilled (page 25),
    peeled, seeded, and finely diced

1 poblano chile, grilled (page 25),
    peeled, seeded, and finely diced

¼ teaspoon red pepper flakes

2 cloves garlic, finely chopped

2 tablespoons finely chopped
    fresh cilantro leaves

¼ teaspoon kosher salt

Nutritional Analysis (per serving)

Calories: **420**   Protein (gm): **40**   Carbohydrates (gm): **7**

Total Sugar (gm): **1**   Total Fat (gm): **27**   Saturated Fat (gm): **3**

Cholesterol (mg): **440**   Sodium (mg): **593**   Fiber (gm): **1**

Mix together all of the ingredients in a medium bowl, cover, and let sit at room temperature for at least 1 hour and up to 2 hours before serving.

GRILLED PRAWNS
24 prawns in the shell, preferably with heads
1 tablespoon olive oil
1 teaspoon kosher salt
1 teaspoon freshly ground black pepper

1. Heat your grill to high.

2. Toss the prawns with the oil in a bowl and season with the salt and pepper. Grill the prawns for 2 to 3 minutes per side until just cooked through. Remove to a platter and immediately spoon the sauce over the prawns with a slotted spoon. Serve hot.

Greek Orzo and Grilled Shrimp Salad with Mustard-Dill Vinaigrette

This is a perfect salad for a warm weather lunch or picnic. Feta and dill are classic Greek flavorings and perfect with shrimp. Although I love the texture that orzo (rice-shaped pasta) adds to the dish, feel free to leave it out if you are really carb phobic; it will still be an awesome salad. Serve this picnic fare in cardboard Chinese take-out containers, which you can find in party supply stores.

Serves 6

ORZO SALAD

1¾ cups orzo

1 large English cucumber, diced

3 green onions, thinly sliced

1 cup grape tomatoes, halved

¼ cup chopped fresh dill

¼ cup white wine vinegar

1 tablespoon Dijon mustard

½ teaspoon kosher salt

¼ teaspoon freshly ground black pepper

½ cup olive oil

8 ounces feta, crumbled

Nutritional Analysis (per serving)

Calories: **531**	Protein (gm): **18**	Carbohydrates (gm): **49**
Total Sugar (gm): **4**	Total Fat (gm): **29**	Saturated Fat (gm): **8.5**
Cholesterol (mg): **62**	Sodium (mg): **795**	Fiber (gm): **2.2**

1. Bring a large pot of salted cold water to a boil. Add the orzo and cook until al dente, 7 to 8 minutes. Drain well.

2. Combine the orzo, cucumber, green onions, and tomatoes in a large bowl.

3. Combine the dill, vinegar, mustard, salt, and pepper in a blender and blend until smooth. With the motor running, slowly drizzle in the olive oil and blend until emulsified. Pour the vinaigrette over the orzo mixture and stir well to combine. Gently fold in the feta cheese. Cover and refrigerate for at least 30 minutes and up to 8 hours.

GRILLED SHRIMP
24 medium shrimp, peeled and deveined
1 tablespoon olive oil
1 teaspoon kosher salt
1 teaspoon freshly ground black pepper
Fresh dill

1. Heat your grill to high.

2. Place the shrimp in a large bowl, toss with the oil, and season with the salt and pepper. Grill for 1½ to 2 minutes per side until just cooked through.

3. Remove the orzo salad from the refrigerator and transfer it to a large platter. Top with the grilled shrimp and garnish with dill before serving.

Grilled Shrimp Escabeche

Escabeche is a Spanish technique for lightly pickling seafood and flavoring it with lots of garlic, chiles, and spices. Like anything that is pickled, this appetizer needs to be made ahead of time so that the grilled shrimp can soak up all the flavors of the savory brine.

Serves 4

1 pound medium shrimp,
    peeled and deveined
$\frac{1}{3}$ cup plus 2 tablespoons olive oil
$\frac{1}{2}$ teaspoon kosher salt
$\frac{1}{2}$ teaspoon freshly ground black pepper
1 large red onion, halved and thinly sliced
4 cloves garlic, thinly sliced
2 serrano chiles, thinly sliced
1 teaspoon cumin seeds
1 teaspoon mustard seeds
2 cups white wine vinegar
2 bay leaves
8 sprigs cilantro, plus 3 tablespoons
    finely chopped cilantro leaves
$\frac{1}{2}$ cup thinly sliced radishes

Nutritional Analysis (per serving)

Calories: **255**   Protein (gm): **25**   Carbohydrates (gm): **10**

Total Sugar (gm): **2**   Total Fat (gm): **12.5**   Saturated Fat (gm): **2**

Cholesterol (mg): **172**   Sodium (mg): **661**   Fiber (gm): **3**

½ **cup green olives, such as Picholine,**
pitted

1. Heat your grill to high.

2. Toss the shrimp in a bowl with 2 tablespoons of the olive oil and the salt and pepper. Grill the shrimp for 1 to 2 minutes per side until just cooked through. Place the shrimp in a medium bowl.

3. Heat the remaining ⅓ cup olive oil in a medium saucepan on top of the grill over high heat. Add the onion, garlic, and chiles and cook, stirring, until soft, 4 to 5 minutes. Add the cumin and mustard seeds and cook for 1 minute. Add the vinegar, bay leaves, and cilantro sprigs and bring to a boil. Remove from the heat, immediately pour over the shrimp, and stir to coat. Let cool to room temperature, then cover and refrigerate for at least 8 hours or overnight, stirring the escabeche a few times during that time.

4. Transfer the escabeche with a slotted spoon to a platter and garnish with the radishes, olives, and chopped cilantro. Serve cold.

Grilled Shrimp in Lettuce Leaves with Serrano-Mint Sauce

These tasty little tacos are wrapped in lettuce leaves, instead of tortillas, in the style of a Vietnamese summer roll. The natural sweetness of the mint plays against the slight heat of the serrano chiles in this Asian-influenced sauce. The contrast of textures is truly great—cool, crisp lettuce surrounds plump, warm shrimp.

Serves 6

SERRANO-MINT SAUCE

½ cup rice vinegar

¼ cup fresh lime juice

3 tablespoons fish sauce

2 tablespoons cold water

1 tablespoon low-sodium soy sauce

1 (1-inch) piece fresh ginger,
    peeled and finely chopped

1 serrano chile, finely diced

2 cloves garlic, finely chopped

2 tablespoons finely chopped
    fresh mint leaves

2 teaspoons sugar

Nutritional Analysis (per serving)

Calories: **163**   Protein (gm): **16**   Carbohydrates (gm): **5**

Total Sugar (gm): **1.6**   Total Fat (gm): **8**   Saturated Fat (gm): **1**

Cholesterol (mg): **115**   Sodium (mg): **814**   Fiber (gm): **1**

Whisk together all of the ingredients in a small bowl, cover, and let sit at room temperature for at least 30 minutes and up to 2 hours before serving.

GRILLED SHRIMP IN LETTUCE

1 pound large shrimp, peeled and deveined

2 tablespoons canola oil

1 teaspoon kosher salt

1 teaspoon freshly ground black pepper

12 Boston lettuce leaves

Fresh cilantro leaves

---

1. Heat your grill to high.

2. Toss the shrimp with the oil and season with the salt and pepper. Grill the shrimp for 1 to 2 minutes per side until just cooked through.

3. Divide the shrimp among the lettuce leaves and drizzle with some of the serrano-mint sauce. Top each serving with a few cilantro leaves, then fold up like a taco and serve immediately.

Grilled Clams on the Half-Shell with Bacon, Garlic, and Hot Pepper

This is my take on that old favorite—clams casino. All the classic flavors are here—smoky bacon, hot red pepper flakes, and a healthy dose of garlic. These clams deliver a spicy kick but nothing you can't handle. And this is a fun one to cook since you can watch the clams pop open when done.

Serves 4

4 ounces (8 strips) bacon, finely diced

6 cloves garlic, finely chopped

½ teaspoon red pepper flakes

2 tablespoons olive oil

**3 tablespoons finely chopped
    flat-leaf parsley leaves**

Freshly ground black pepper

36 littleneck clams, scrubbed

1. Heat your grill to medium.

2. Place a medium sauté pan on the grill, add the bacon and cook until light golden brown, 4 to 5 minutes. Add the garlic and red pepper flakes and continue cooking until

---

Nutritional Analysis (per serving)

Calories: **299**   Protein (gm): **24**   Carbohydrates (gm): **5**

Total Sugar (gm): **0**   Total Fat (gm): **20**   Saturated Fat (gm): **5**

Cholesterol (mg): **71**   Sodium (mg): **656**   Fiber (gm): **0**

the bacon is crisp, 2 to 3 minutes. Remove from the heat, stir in the olive oil and parsley, and season with black pepper to taste.

3. Increase the heat of the grill to high. Place the clams directly on the grates of the grill, close the cover, and cook until all of the clams have opened, 3 to 4 minutes (discard any that are not).

4. Remove the clams to a platter and top each with some of the bacon mixture before serving.

Grilled Oysters with Mango Pico de Gallo and Red Chile Horseradish

I was taught to grill oysters on one of my trips to the Pacific Northwest. This is one of those dishes where organization is imperative. Because the oysters cook for only a few minutes, you've got to have the garnishes ready before you put the shells on the grill. The mango pico de gallo and the red chile horseradish are hot and sweet on your tongue. If you think that the red chile horseradish looks too spicy, don't worry, for the sweet mango provides just the right cooling sensation. The oysters actually "pop" when they are cooked and make for a great presentation.

Serves 4

MANGO PICO DE GALLO

1 ripe mango, peeled, pitted, and finely diced

½ small red onion, finely diced

1 jalapeño chile, finely diced

Juice of 1 lime

2 tablespoons olive oil

1 tablespoon finely chopped fresh cilantro leaves

2 teaspoons honey

¼ teaspoon kosher salt

¼ teaspoon freshly ground black pepper

Nutritional Analysis (per serving with 2 tablespoons pico de gallo)

Calories: **203**	Protein (gm): **9**	Carbohydrates (gm): **22**
Total Sugar (gm): **13**	Total Fat (gm): **10**	Saturated Fat (gm): **1.8**
Cholesterol (mg): **59**	Sodium (mg): **375**	Fiber (gm): **3**

Combine all of the ingredients in a medium bowl and let sit at room temperature for at least 30 minutes and up to 1 hour.

RED CHILE HORSERADISH
¼ cup prepared horseradish, drained
1 tablespoon ancho chile powder

Stir together the ingredients in a small bowl.

GRILLED OYSTERS
32 oysters, such as Blue Point or Malpeque, scrubbed

1. Heat your grill to high.

2. Place the oysters directly on the grates of the grill, close the cover, and cook until all of the oysters have opened, 4 to 5 minutes (discarding any that are not).

3. Top each oyster with 1 teaspoon pico de gallo and ¼ teaspoon red chile horseradish. Serve hot.

Cumin Grilled Sea Scallops with Chickpea Salad and Red Pepper–Tahini Vinaigrette

Grilled peppers add a sweetness and smokiness to this vinaigrette, while tahini gives it a creamy consistency. Cumin and chickpeas are fantastic together, and a little cumin goes a long way.

Serves 6

CHICKPEA SALAD
¼ cup fresh lemon juice

¼ cup olive oil

1 teaspoon ground cumin

½ teaspoon cayenne

¼ teaspoon kosher salt

¼ teaspoon freshly ground black pepper

2 (16-ounce) cans chickpeas, rinsed and drained

2 serrano chiles, grilled (page 25), peeled, seeded, and thinly sliced lengthwise

1 large yellow bell pepper, seeded and finely diced

¼ cup finely chopped flat-leaf parsley leaves

¼ cup finely chopped chives

Nutritional Analysis (per serving)

Calories: **860**	Protein (gm): **37**	Carbohydrates (gm): **75**
Total Sugar (gm): **16**	Total Fat (gm): **47**	Saturated Fat (gm): **6**
Cholesterol (mg): **30**	Sodium (mg): **584**	Fiber (gm): **20**

Whisk together the lemon juice, oil, cumin, cayenne, salt, and pepper in a large bowl. Add the remaining ingredients and stir well to combine. Transfer the salad to a large serving platter, cover, and let sit at room temperature for at least 30 minutes and up to 2 hours before serving.

RED PEPPER-TAHINI VINAIGRETTE

¼ cup sherry vinegar
Pinch of saffron
2 red bell peppers, grilled (page 25), peeled, seeded, and chopped
2 cloves garlic, chopped
2 tablespoons tahini
2 teaspoons honey
¼ cup cold water
¼ teaspoon kosher salt
¼ teaspoon freshly ground black pepper
½ cup olive oil

1. Combine the vinegar and saffron in a small bowl and let sit for 5 minutes to allow the saffron to bloom.

2. Transfer the mixture to a blender. Add the red peppers, garlic, tahini, honey, water, salt, and pepper and blend until smooth. With the motor running, slowly drizzle in the oil and blend until emulsified. *The vinaigrette can be made up to 4 hours in advance, covered, and kept refrigerated. Bring to room temperature before serving.*

CUMIN GRILLED SEA SCALLOPS

24 large sea scallops
1 tablespoon olive oil
2 teaspoons ground cumin
1 tablespoon kosher salt
1 teaspoon freshly ground black pepper

1. Heat your grill to high.

2. Brush the scallops on both sides with the oil. Mix together the cumin, salt, and pepper in a small bowl and season each scallop with the mixture. Grill the scallops until crusty, golden brown, and just cooked through, 2 to 3 minutes on each side.

3. Top the chickpea salad with the scallops and drizzle with the vinaigrette before serving.

**Smoky and Fiery Skirt Steak
with Avocado-Oregano Relish (page 166)**

Grilled Chicken Breasts with Fontina and Prosciutto with Sage-Orange Vinaigrette (page 122) and Grilled Figs with Vanilla-Orange Crème Fraîche and Toasted Pistachios (page 190)

From bottom: Grilled Turkey Burgers
with Monterey Jack, Poblano Pickle Relish,
and Avocado Mayonnaise (page 132);
Lamb Burgers with Tomato-Mint Salsa
and Feta Cheese (page 172);
and Green Chile Burgers
(page 156)

Grilled Oysters with Mango Pico de Gallo
and Red Chile Horseradish (page 78)
and Grilled Clams on the Half-Shell with
Bacon, Garlic, and Hot Pepper (page 76)

Clockwise from top: Bulgur Salad
with Green Onion Vinaigrette (page 50),
Grilled Asparagus and Egg Salad
with Tarragon-Caper Vinaigrette (page 30),
and Red Cabbage and Beet Slaw (page 48)

Cumin Grilled Sea Scallops with Chickpea Salad and Red Pepper–Tahini Vinaigrette (page 80)

Pork Tenderloin Crusted with Green Onion, Jalapeño, and Ginger (page 144)

Grilled Lamb Chops
and Oregano Vinaigrette
with Radish Tzatziki (page 170)
and Pomegranate Margarita (page 184)

Grilled Sea Scallops with Avocado Vinaigrette and Jalapeño Pesto

Plump sea scallops, creamy avocados, and spicy jalapeños create a great combination of flavor and textures. Don't shy away from avocados because they are high in calories, for they are also rich in good, heart-healthy fat, vitamin E, and potassium.

Serves 6

JALAPEÑO PESTO

1½ cups fresh cilantro leaves

6 jalapeños chiles, grilled (page 25), peeled, and chopped

1 clove garlic, chopped

1 tablespoon pine nuts

¼ teaspoon kosher salt

⅛ teaspoon freshly ground black pepper

½ cup olive oil

Combine the cilantro, jalapeños, garlic, pine nuts, salt, and pepper in a food processor or blender and process until smooth. With the motor running, drizzle in the oil and process until emulsified. Scrape the mixture into a bowl and set aside. *The pesto can be*

Nutritional Analysis (per serving with 2 tablespoons vinaigrette)

Calories: **377**	Protein (gm): **27**	Carbohydrates (gm): **12**
Total Sugar (gm): **2.5**	Total Fat (gm): **25**	Saturated Fat (gm): **2.8**
Cholesterol (mg): **50**	Sodium (mg): **487**	Fiber (gm): **4.5**

made up to 2 days in advance, covered, and kept refrigerated. Bring to room temperature before serving.

AVOCADO VINAIGRETTE

1 ripe avocado, halved, pitted, peeled, and chopped

½ cup fresh lime juice

2 tablespoons water

3 tablespoons chopped red onion

2 teaspoons honey

¼ teaspoon ground cumin

¼ teaspoon kosher salt

¼ teaspoon freshly ground black pepper

¼ cup canola oil

Combine the avocado, lime juice, water, onion, honey, cumin, salt, and pepper in a blender and blend until smooth. With the motor running, slowly drizzle in the oil and blend until emulsified. If the mixture is too thick and does not pour easily, add additional water to thin it to a pourable consistency.

SEA SCALLOPS

24 large sea scallops

2 tablespoons olive oil

1 teaspoon kosher salt

1 teaspoon freshly ground black pepper

---

1. Heat your grill to high.

2. Brush the scallops on both sides with the oil and season with the salt and pepper. Grill the scallops until crusty, golden brown, and just cooked through, 2 to 3 minutes per side.

3. Serve 4 scallops per person on each plate. Drizzle 2 tablespoons of the avocado vinaigrette over the scallops and top each scallop with a teaspoon of the jalapeño pesto.

Grilled Lobster Tails
with Hot Ginger–Green Onion Vinaigrette

Yes, lobster tails are truly decadent, but without the butter normally served alongside them, lobster is low in calories and full of protein. With its fiery touch of ginger, this refreshing vinaigrette keeps the dish from overpowering richness. Warming the vinaigrette brings out its flavors, while its intensity enhances the sweet flavor of the lobster tails.

Serves 4

GRILLED LOBSTER

**4 lobster tails, 10 to 12 ounces each,
    thawed if frozen, shelled**

**Eight 10-inch wooden skewers,
    soaked in water for 30 minutes**

4 teaspoons canola oil

¼ teaspoon kosher salt

½ teaspoon freshly ground black pepper

1. Heat your grill to high.

2. Thread each lobster tail lengthwise onto 2 skewers so that the meat lies flat. Brush the tails with the oil and season with the salt and pepper. Grill for 4 to 5 minutes on each side until slightly charred and just cooked through.

Nutritional Analysis (per serving)

Calories: **407**   Protein (gm): **54**   Carbohydrates (gm): **4**

Total Sugar (gm): **0**   Total Fat (gm): **18**   Saturated Fat (gm): **2.6**

Cholesterol (mg): **270**   Sodium (mg): **1,012**   Fiber (gm): **0**

HOT GINGER–GREEN ONION VINAIGRETTE

¼ cup peanut oil

3 tablespoons finely chopped fresh ginger

2 cloves garlic, finely chopped

1 Thai or red jalapeño chile, finely chopped,
     or 1 teaspoon red pepper flakes

½ cup rice vinegar

1 tablespoon low-sodium soy sauce

¼ teaspoon sugar

2 teaspoons toasted sesame oil

4 green onions, light and dark parts, thinly sliced

1 tablespoon sesame seeds, toasted (page 26)

1. While the lobster is grilling, heat the oil in a medium saucepan on the grate of the grill or on your stovetop. Add the ginger, garlic, and chile and cook, stirring occasionally, until soft, about 5 minutes. Add the vinegar, soy sauce, and sugar and bring to a simmer. Remove from the heat and stir in the sesame oil and green onions.

2. Arrange the grilled tails on a platter, drizzle with the hot vinaigrette, and sprinkle with the sesame seeds before serving.

SKEWERS

I prefer using wooden skewers for my recipes. I find that metal skewers, which hold the heat, are often too hot to handle straight off the grill. If you are using wooden skewers, it is important that you soak them first in water for at least 30 minutes to prevent them from burning on the grill.

"Barbecued" Mahimahi
with Yellow Pepper–Cilantro Pesto

The spice rub not only adds an earthy BBQ taste to the fish but also creates a great crust. Serve just a dollop of the pesto right on top to add extra flavor to the fish, as well as cool the barbecue rub.

Serves 4

"BARBECUE" RUB

2 tablespoons Spanish paprika

1 tablespoon ancho chile powder

2 teaspoons ground cumin

2 teaspoons dark brown sugar

1 teaspoon chile de árbol powder

1 teaspoon kosher salt

1 teaspoon coarsely ground black pepper

Stir together all of the ingredients in a small bowl.

Nutritional Analysis (per serving)

Calories: **474**   Protein (gm): **46**   Carbohydrates (gm): **12.5**

Total Sugar (gm): **4.5**   Total Fat (gm): **27**   Saturated Fat (gm): **4**

Cholesterol (mg): **168**   Sodium (mg): **643**   Fiber (gm): **4**

YELLOW PEPPER–CILANTRO PESTO

2 yellow bell peppers, grilled (page 25),
   peeled, seeded, and chopped

1 clove garlic, chopped

2 tablespoons pine nuts

¼ cup chopped fresh cilantro leaves

3 tablespoons grated Parmesan cheese

¼ cup olive oil

¼ teaspoon kosher salt

¼ teaspoon freshly ground black pepper

Combine the peppers, garlic, pine nuts, cilantro, and Parmesan in a food processor or blender and process until combined. With the motor running, slowly drizzle in the oil and process until emulsified. Season with the salt and pepper.

MAHIMAHI

4 skinless mahimahi fillets, 8 ounces each

4 teaspoons olive oil

Cilantro leaves

1. Heat your grill to high.

2. Brush each fillet on both sides with the oil. Rub 1 side of each fillet with a heaping tablespoon of the barbecue rub. Place rub side down on the grill and cook until slightly charred and a crust has formed, 2 to 3 minutes. Turn the fish over and grill for 3 to 4 minutes longer until cooked to medium (page 12). Remove from the grill and let rest for 5 minutes.

3. Top each fillet with pesto and garnish with cilantro leaves before serving.

Grilled Halibut with Grilled Eggplant Salad

This is really two dishes on one plate. The halibut is grilled simply and should be drizzled with your best extra-virgin olive oil. The grilled eggplant salad is done in the style of a Sicilian caponata. It is a riot of flavors, sweet and sour from the raisins and vinegar, salty from the capers and olives, with some red pepper flakes for heat and pine nuts for crunch. It's awesome!

Serves 4

GRILLED EGGPLANT SALAD

1 medium eggplant, cut lengthwise into
   ½-inch-thick slices
1 large red onion, cut into ½-inch-thick slices
4 plum tomatoes, halved
½ cup olive oil
1 teaspoon kosher salt
1 teaspoon freshly ground black pepper
¼ cup green olives, pitted and chopped
2 tablespoons capers, drained
2 tablespoons golden raisins
2 tablespoons pine nuts, toasted (page 26)
3 cloves garlic, finely chopped
¼ teaspoon red pepper flakes
¼ cup red wine vinegar

Nutritional Analysis (per serving)

Calories: **547**	Protein (gm): **51**	Carbohydrates (gm): **25**
Total Sugar (gm): **11**	Total Fat (gm): **28**	Saturated Fat (gm): **3.6**
Cholesterol (mg): **73**	Sodium (mg): **690**	Fiber (gm): **8**

2 teaspoons honey

¼ cup finely chopped flat-leaf parsley leaves

1. Heat your grill to high. Brush the eggplant, onion slices, and tomatoes with ¼ cup of the olive oil and season each type of vegetable with ¼ teaspoon of the salt and ¼ teaspoon of the pepper.

2. Grill the eggplant for 6 to 8 minutes per side until golden brown and cooked through. Grill the onions for 3 to 4 minutes per side until golden brown and just cooked through. Grill the tomatoes for 2 minutes per side until charred and slightly soft.

3. Remove the vegetables from the grill and cut into ½-inch pieces. Place the vegetables in a medium bowl and add the olives, capers, raisins, and pine nuts.

4. Mix together the garlic, red pepper flakes, vinegar, and honey in a small bowl and season with the remaining ¼ teaspoon salt and ¼ teaspoon pepper. Slowly drizzle in the remaining ¼ cup olive oil and whisk until emulsified.

5. Pour the dressing over the vegetables, add the parsley, and stir gently to combine. Let the salad sit at room temperature for at least 30 minutes and up to 2 hours before serving.

GRILLED HALIBUT

4 skinless halibut fillets, 8 ounces each

4 teaspoons olive oil

1 teaspoon kosher salt

1 teaspoon freshly ground black pepper

1. Heat your grill to high.

2. Brush each halibut fillet on both sides with the oil and season with the salt and the pepper. Grill for 3 to 4 minutes per side until cooked to medium (page 12). Remove the fish from the grill and let rest for 5 minutes.

3. Top the fillets with the grilled eggplant salad before serving.

Yucatán Marinated Halibut in Banana Leaves with Pineapple-Orange Relish

BOBBY FLAY'S GRILLING FOR LIFE

Think of this healthy cooking technique as the Cuban version of the classic French technique of cooking fish wrapped in paper, fish *en papillote.* The banana leaves impart a wonderfully herbaceous taste to the fish while, in essence, steaming the fish on the grill. Banana leaves can be found in Latin markets and online at www.melissas.com. Note: Tell your guests not to eat the banana leaves.

Serves 4

PINEAPPLE-ORANGE RELISH

Juice of 2 limes

2 tablespoons fresh orange juice

2 tablespoons olive oil

¼ teaspoon chile de árbol powder

½ ripe pineapple, peeled, cored, and cut into small dice

2 oranges, segmented (page 26)

3 green onions, white and light green parts, thinly sliced

3 tablespoons chopped fresh mint leaves

¼ teaspoon kosher salt

Nutritional Analysis (per serving)

Calories: **297**   Protein (gm): **48**   Carbohydrates (gm): **6**

Total Sugar (gm): **3**   Total Fat (gm): **8**   Saturated Fat (gm): **1**

Cholesterol (mg): **72**   Sodium (mg): **425**   Fiber (gm): **1**

Whisk together the lime juice, orange juice, oil, and chile powder in a medium bowl. Add the remaining ingredients and stir to combine. Let sit at room temperature for at least 30 minutes and up to 4 hours before serving.

MARINATED HALIBUT
¼ cup fresh orange juice
¼ cup fresh lime juice
¼ cup fresh lemon juice
2 tablespoons olive oil
1 tablespoon ancho chile powder
1 tablespoon pasilla chile powder
2 teaspoons chile de árbol powder
¼ teaspoon ground cumin
1 teaspoon kosher salt
½ teaspoon freshly ground black pepper
4 skinless halibut fillets, 8 ounces each
4 banana leaves, soaked in water for at least
    30 minutes

1. Heat your grill to high.

2. Whisk together the citrus juices, oil, chile powders, cumin, salt, and pepper in a large shallow baking dish. Add the halibut fillets and turn to coat. Marinate for 5 minutes.

3. Remove the banana leaves from the water and shake off the excess water. Lay the leaves on a flat surface and place 1 fillet in the center of each leaf. Fold the banana leaf loosely around each fillet. Place the packets seam side down on the grill, close the cover, and grill for 8 to 10 minutes until cooked to medium (page 12). Use a wide metal spatula to carefully remove the packets from the grill and let rest for 5 minutes.

4. Open the packets and serve the fish on the banana leaves if desired. Top each fillet with pineapple-orange relish before serving.

Grilled Jerk-Rubbed Grouper with Hot Vinegar Sauce

Any trip to the Caribbean has to include some great jerk. Get ready for some flavor! This preparation is also good with snapper, bass, and other meaty fish, such as swordfish and shark.

Serves 4

HOT VINEGAR SAUCE

1 tablespoon canola oil

1 medium yellow onion, halved
    and thinly sliced

2 cloves garlic, chopped

½ Scotch bonnet chile, finely chopped

1¼ cups white wine vinegar

1 teaspoon fennel seeds

3 allspice berries

1 teaspoon sugar

¼ teaspoon kosher salt

1 tablespoon chopped fresh thyme leaves

2 tablespoons chopped fresh flat-leaf
    parsley leaves

Nutritional Analysis (per serving)

Calories: **307**   Protein (gm): **47**   Carbohydrates (gm): **17**

Total Sugar (gm): **6**   Total Fat (gm): **5**   Saturated Fat (gm): **0**

Cholesterol (mg): **56**   Sodium (mg): **876**   Fiber (gm): **4**

Heat the oil in a medium saucepan over medium-high heat. Add the onion, garlic, and chile and cook until soft, 4 to 5 minutes. Add the vinegar, fennel, allspice, sugar, and salt, bring to a simmer, and cook for 10 minutes. Strain the sauce into a bowl and stir in the thyme and parsley. Cover and keep warm while you prepare the fish.

JERK-RUBBED GROUPER

2 tablespoons light brown sugar

1 tablespoon ground coriander

1 tablespoon ground ginger

1 tablespoon habanero chile powder

1 teaspoon onion powder

1 teaspoon garlic powder

1 teaspoon dried thyme

1 teaspoon kosher salt

2 teaspoons coarsely ground black pepper

1 teaspoon ground cinnamon

1 teaspoon ground allspice

1 teaspoon ground cloves

4 skinless grouper fillets, 8 ounces each

1. Heat your grill to medium-high.

2. Combine the sugar, spices, and seasonings in a medium bowl. Rub both sides of the fish fillets with the rub and grill for 4 to 5 minutes per side until cooked to medium (page 12).

3. Remove the fish from the grill, place on a platter, and immediately spoon the warm vinegar sauce over the fish. Let rest for 5 minutes before serving.

Grilled Red Snapper
with Grapefruit-Thyme Mojo

Grapefruit is a great lower-in-carb alternative to oranges, which have a higher sugar content. This mojo makes use of grapefruit juice and zest in a sweet-tart Latin sauce that is wonderful with flaky white fish like snapper.

Serves 4

GRAPEFRUIT-THYME MOJO

¼ **cup olive oil**

8 **cloves garlic, roasted (page 25)**

½ **cup fresh grapefruit juice**

¼ **cup fresh orange juice**

2 **teaspoons grated grapefruit zest**

1 **serrano chile, coarsely chopped**

1 **tablespoon chopped fresh thyme leaves**

¼ **teaspoon kosher salt**

Combine all of the ingredients in a blender and blend until smooth.

Nutritional Analysis (per serving)

Calories: **398**   Protein (gm): **48**   Carbohydrates (gm): **9**

Total Sugar (gm): **4**   Total Fat (gm): **19**   Saturated Fat (gm): **3**

Cholesterol (mg): **84**   Sodium (mg): **545**   Fiber (gm): **1**

GRILLED RED SNAPPER

4 skinless red snapper fillets, 8 ounces each

1 teaspoon kosher salt

½ teaspoon freshly ground black pepper

Fresh thyme leaves

Grilled grapefruit wedges (page 26)

1. Heat your grill to high.

2. Place the fish in a large shallow baking dish, pour half of the mojo over, and turn to coat. Cover and let marinate for 10 minutes.

3. Remove the fish from the marinade and season both sides with the salt and pepper. Place the fish on the grill and grill for 3 to 4 minutes until golden brown and slightly charred. Turn the fish over and continue grilling for 3 to 4 minutes for medium (page 12), brushing with the remaining mojo. Remove the fish from the grill and let rest for 5 minutes.

4. Serve the snapper garnished with fresh thyme leaves and grilled grapefruit wedges.

Grilled Red Snapper
with Green Romesco Sauce

At my Spanish restaurant, Bolo, we came up with a green romesco sauce, a play on the classic romesco, which is made with red peppers and tomatoes. Think of it as the Spanish answer to Italy's pesto. The toasted almond garnish adds crunch to the dish.

Serves 4

GREEN ROMESCO SAUCE

2 tablespoons olive oil

6 cloves garlic, peeled

¼ cup blanched almonds, toasted (page 26)

2 poblano chiles, grilled (page 25),
**   peeled, seeded, and chopped**

1 green bell pepper, grilled (page 25),
**   peeled, seeded, and chopped**

½ cup white wine vinegar

¼ cup water

¼ cup chopped fresh flat-leaf parsley leaves

1 tablespoon honey

¼ teaspoon kosher salt

¼ teaspoon freshly ground black pepper

Nutritional Analysis (per serving with 2 tablespoons sauce)

Calories: **380**   Protein (gm): **48**   Carbohydrates (gm): **10**

Total Sugar (gm): **4**   Total Fat (gm): **16**   Saturated Fat (gm): **1.7**

Cholesterol (mg): **56**   Sodium (mg): **123**   Fiber (gm): **2**

1. Heat the olive oil in a large sauté pan over medium-high heat. Add the garlic and cook until soft and light golden brown, 4 to 5 minutes. Stir in the almonds, poblanos, and bell pepper and cook for 1 minute. Using a slotted spoon, transfer to a food processor or blender.

2. Add the vinegar to the pan, simmer for 1 minute, and add it to the food processor along with the water, parsley, and honey. Process the mixture until smooth, then season with the salt and pepper. If the mixture is too thick, add water to thin it to a sauce consistency.

GRILLED RED SNAPPER
**4 skinless red snapper fillets,
8 ounces each**
4 teaspoons olive oil
1 tablespoon Spanish paprika
$\frac{1}{4}$ teaspoon kosher salt
$\frac{1}{4}$ teaspoon freshly ground black pepper
**2 tablespoons sliced blanched almonds,
toasted (page 26)**
Chopped fresh flat-leaf parsley leaves

1. Heat your grill to high.

2. Brush the snapper fillets with the oil and season on one side with the paprika, salt, and pepper. Grill the fish seasoned side down until slightly charred and a crust has formed, 3 to 4 minutes. Turn the fish over and continue grilling for 3 to 4 minutes until cooked to medium (page 12).

3. Top each fillet with 2 tablespoons of the romesco and garnish with the almonds and parsley leaves. Serve with the remaining romesco sauce if desired.

Grilled Salmon with Anchovy Vinaigrette and Grilled Pepper and Black Olive Relish

Too many people are afraid of anchovies. These little fish have gotten a bad rap, but they really are a seasoning miracle. Their pungent saltiness lends an incredible layer of flavor to this vinaigrette. With the relish, the vinaigrette provides the perfect balance for the rich, buttery salmon.

Serves 4

GRILLED PEPPER AND BLACK OLIVE RELISH

2 red bell peppers, grilled (page 25), peeled, seeded, and diced

2 yellow bell peppers, grilled (page 25), peeled, seeded, and diced

½ cup coarsely chopped pitted Niçoise olives

1 tablespoon minced garlic

¼ cup coarsely chopped fresh flat-leaf parsley leaves

1 tablespoon chopped fresh thyme leaves

¼ cup sherry vinegar

2 teaspoons honey

1 teaspoon kosher salt

1 teaspoon freshly ground black pepper

Nutritional Analysis (per serving with 2 tablespoons vinaigrette)

Calories: **373**	Protein (gm): **36**	Carbohydrates (gm): **10**
Total Sugar (gm): **6.5**	Total Fat (gm): **20**	Saturated Fat (gm): **3**
Cholesterol (mg): **94**	Sodium (mg): **765**	Fiber (gm): **3**

Combine the peppers, olives, garlic, parsley, thyme, vinegar, and honey in a mixing bowl. Season with the salt and pepper. *The relish can be made up to 1 day in advance. Bring to room temperature before serving.*

ANCHOVY VINAIGRETTE

2 tablespoons mayonnaise

2 teaspoons Dijon mustard

1 teaspoon fresh lemon juice

¼ cup sherry vinegar

¼ teaspoon freshly ground black pepper

5 anchovy fillets

1 small shallot, coarsely chopped

⅓ cup olive oil

Combine the mayonnaise, mustard, lemon juice, vinegar, pepper, anchovies, and shallot in a blender and blend until smooth. With the motor running, drizzle in the oil and blend until emulsified. *The vinaigrette can be made up to 8 hours in advance and kept refrigerated.*

GRILLED SALMON

4 skinless salmon fillets, 6 ounces each

1 tablespoon olive oil

¼ teaspoon kosher salt

1 teaspoon freshly ground black pepper

1. Heat your grill to high.

2. Brush the salmon fillets on both sides with the oil and season with the salt and pepper. Place the fillets on the grill and cook until golden brown and a crust has formed, 2 to 3 minutes. Turn the salmon over and continue grilling for 3 to 4 minutes until cooked to medium (page 12). Remove from the grill and let rest for 5 minutes.

3. Drizzle each fillet with 2 tablespoons of the vinaigrette and top with the relish. Serve the remaining vinaigrette on the side if desired.

Grilled Salmon with Lemon, Dill, and Caper Vinaigrette

These flavors are classic accompaniments for salmon. The capers have a salty flavor that adds just the right touch to the fresh lemon zest and dill. Be sure to spoon the vinaigrette over the salmon as it comes off the grill so that the vinaigrette penetrates the fillets.

Serves 4

LEMON-DILL VINAIGRETTE
2 tablespoons white wine vinegar

2 tablespoons fresh lemon juice

2 teaspoons grated lemon zest

3 tablespoons chopped fresh dill

1 teaspoon honey

⅛ teaspoon kosher salt

¼ teaspoon freshly ground black pepper

⅓ cup olive oil

2 tablespoons capers, drained

Combine the vinegar, lemon juice, zest, dill, honey, salt, and pepper in a blender and blend until smooth. With the motor running, slowly add the oil and blend until emulsified. Pour the vinaigrette into a small bowl and stir in the capers.

Nutritional Analysis (per serving with 2 tablespoons vinaigrette)

Calories: **469**   Protein (gm): **34**   Carbohydrates (gm): **1**

Total Sugar (gm): **0**   Total Fat (gm): **35**   Saturated Fat (gm): **5**

Cholesterol (mg): **93**   Sodium (mg): **247**   Fiber (gm): **0**

GRILLED SALMON

4 skinless salmon fillets, 6 ounces each

4 teaspoons olive oil

¼ teaspoon kosher salt

¼ teaspoon freshly ground black pepper

Fresh dill sprigs

1. Heat your grill to high.

2. Brush the salmon fillets on both sides with the oil and season with the salt and pepper. Place the fillets on the grill and cook until golden brown and a crust has formed, 2 to 3 minutes. Flip the salmon over and continue grilling for 3 to 4 minutes until cooked to medium (page 12).

3. Remove to a platter, spoon 2 tablespoons vinaigrette over each fillet, and let rest for 5 minutes. Garnish with dill sprigs. Serve the remaining vinaigrette on the side if desired.

Whole Sea Bass
with Charred Serrano–Basil Vinaigrette

BOBBY
FLAY'S
GRILLING
FOR
LIFE

104

A grilled whole fish is an impressive sight. Beyond that, grilling the fish whole ensures a great contrast of textures—the fish will be tender on the inside and crispy on the outside.

Serves 4

CHARRED SERRANO-BASIL VINAIGRETTE

2 serrano chiles, grilled (page 25), peeled, seeded, and chopped

3 tablespoons diced red onion

3 cloves garlic, finely chopped

1 tablespoon Dijon mustard

¼ cup rice vinegar

1 tablespoon balsamic vinegar

¼ teaspoon kosher salt

¼ teaspoon freshly ground black pepper

½ cup olive oil

2 tablespoons finely chopped fresh basil leaves

Combine the chiles, onion, garlic, mustard, both vinegars, salt, and pepper in a blender and blend until smooth. With the motor running, slowly drizzle in the oil and blend until emulsified. Pour into a bowl and stir in the chopped basil.

Nutritional Analysis (per serving)

Calories: **455**	Protein (gm): **43**	Carbohydrates (gm): **3.5**
Total Sugar (gm): **1**	Total Fat (gm): **30**	Saturated Fat (gm): **4.5**
Cholesterol (mg): **93**	Sodium (mg): **823**	Fiber (gm): **1**

GRILLED SEA BASS

4 whole sea bass, 1 pound each, scaled and gutted, head and tail intact

2 tablespoons olive oil

2 teaspoons kosher salt

2 teaspoons freshly ground black pepper

1 bunch fresh basil

1. Heat your grill to medium-high.

2. Brush both sides of each fish with the oil and season inside and out with the salt and pepper. Stuff the cavity of each fish with some of the basil. Grill the fish until slightly charred on one side, 4 to 5 minutes. Using a heavy-duty spatula, carefully turn the fish over, close the cover, and continue grilling until just cooked through, 6 to 7 minutes longer.

3. Remove the fish from the grill and immediately drizzle with the vinaigrette. Let rest for 5 minutes before serving.

Grilled Brook Trout with Horseradish and Tarragon Tartar Sauce

BOBBY
FLAY'S
GRILLING
FOR
LIFE

106

This tartar sauce is killer! The assertive horseradish and fresh lemon zest are perfect contrasts to the mild, sweet flavor of flaky brook trout. Be sure to prepare the tartar sauce in advance for the flavors need at least 2 hours to meld. This sauce is most flavorful at room temperature, so be sure to take it out of the refrigerator at least 30 minutes before serving.

Serves 4

HORSERADISH AND TARRAGON TARTAR SAUCE

⅓ **cup mayonnaise**

1 **teaspoon grated lemon zest**

3 **tablespoons prepared horseradish, drained**

2 **tablespoons finely chopped red onion**

2 **tablespoons capers, drained**

3 **dashes Tabasco sauce**

2 **tablespoons finely chopped fresh tarragon leaves**

¼ **teaspoon kosher salt**

¼ **teaspoon freshly ground black pepper**

Nutritional Analysis (per serving)

Calories: **507**   Protein (gm): **47**   Carbohydrates (gm): **1**

Total Sugar (gm): **0**   Total Fat (gm): **33**   Saturated Fat (gm): **4.8**

Cholesterol (mg): **138**   Sodium (mg): **661**   Fiber (gm): **0**

Combine all of the ingredients in a medium bowl. Cover and refrigerate for at least 2 hours and up to 8 hours. Bring to room temperature before serving.

GRILLED BROOK TROUT

4 trout fillets, 8 ounces each

1 tablespoon canola oil

1 teaspoon kosher salt

½ teaspoon freshly ground black pepper

---

1. Heat your grill to high.

2. Brush the fillets with the oil and season on both sides with the salt and pepper. Grill for 3 to 4 minutes on each side until golden brown and cooked to medium (page 12). Remove from the grill and let rest for 5 minutes.

3. Top each fillet with tartar sauce before serving.

Grilled Tuna with White Bean Salad

This is a dish you would find in Tuscany or a great tapas bar in Spain. Be sure to cook the beans long enough—you want them to be creamy.

Serves 6

**BOBBY
FLAY'S
GRILLING
FOR
LIFE**

108

WHITE BEAN SALAD

12 ounces dried white beans, picked over,
   soaked in water overnight, and drained
1 small yellow onion, quartered
1 medium carrot, cut into 4 pieces
3 cloves garlic, smashed
1 bay leaf
2 tablespoons olive oil
3 tablespoons balsamic vinegar
1 red onion, halved and thinly sliced
1 tablespoon chopped fresh thyme leaves
1 teaspoon kosher salt
¼ teaspoon red pepper flakes

1. Put the beans in a large pot and add the onion, carrot, garlic, bay leaf, and enough cold water to cover by 2 inches. Bring to a boil, then lower the heat so that the water simmers.

Nutritional Analysis (per serving)

Calories: **382**	Protein (gm): **42**	Carbohydrates (gm): **21**
Total Sugar (gm): **3.7**	Total Fat (gm): **14**	Saturated Fat (gm): **2.7**
Cholesterol (mg): **57**	Sodium (mg): **450**	Fiber (gm): **5**

Cook until the beans are soft, 1 to 1½ hours. Drain the beans and pick out the onion, carrot, garlic, and bay leaf.

2. Place the beans in a bowl and toss with the oil and vinegar. Fold in the red onion and thyme and season with the salt and red pepper flakes. Cover and let sit at room temperature while you prepare the tuna.

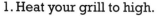

GRILLED TUNA AND RADICCHIO
4 tuna steaks, 8 ounces each
3 teaspoons olive oil
1 teaspoon kosher salt
1 teaspoon freshly ground black pepper
1 head radicchio, halved
¼ cup coarsely chopped fresh
flat-leaf parsley leaves

1. Heat your grill to high.

2. Brush the tuna steaks on both sides with 2 teaspoons of the oil and season with the salt and pepper. Place on the grill and cook for 2 to 3 minutes per side until slightly charred and cooked to medium-rare (page 12).

3. Remove from the grill and transfer to a cutting board. Let rest for 5 minutes before cutting into ¼-inch-thick slices.

4. Brush the cut sides of the radicchio with the remaining 1 teaspoon oil and grill cut side down until slightly charred and wilted, about 2 minutes.

5. Remove the radicchio from the grill and cut into ¼-inch-thick slices. Stir the radicchio into the white beans.

6. Transfer the beans to a platter and top with the sliced tuna. Sprinkle with the parsley. Serve warm or at room temperature.

Grilled Tuna Salad Sandwiches with Lemon-Habanero Mayonnaise

BOBBY
FLAY'S
GRILLING
FOR
LIFE

110

This is definitely not the tuna salad sandwich you packed for school. This grown-up sandwich makes a perfect summer lunchtime meal. Canned tuna may have its time and place, but nothing beats the real thing for its meaty texture and fresh taste. The habanero is very spicy, but the cool mayo and the acidic lemon temper the chile, taking you past the heat so that all you taste is the chile's true flavor.

Serves 6

LEMON-HABANERO MAYONNAISE

¾ cup mayonnaise

2 tablespoons fresh lemon juice

2 teaspoons grated lemon zest

½ habanero chile, chopped

¼ teaspoon kosher salt

¼ teaspoon freshly ground black pepper

1 small red onion, finely chopped

1 large rib celery, finely chopped

2 tablespoons chopped fresh
    flat-leaf parsley leaves

Nutritional Analysis (per serving)

Calories: **587**   Protein (gm): **61**   Carbohydrates (gm): **33**

Total Sugar (gm): **2.5**   Total Fat (gm): **26**   Saturated Fat (gm): **4.5**

Cholesterol (mg): **90**   Sodium (mg): **576**   Fiber (gm): **8**

Combine the mayonnaise, lemon juice, zest, and chile in a blender and blend until smooth. Season with the salt and pepper and transfer to a large bowl. Stir in the onion, celery, and parsley. Set aside while you prepare the tuna.

GRILLED TUNA SALAD SANDWICHES
4 tuna steaks, 8 ounces each
2 teaspoons olive oil
1 teaspoon kosher salt
1 teaspoon freshly ground black pepper
12 slices seven-grain bread
1 small bunch watercress

---

1. Heat your grill to high.

2. Brush the tuna steaks with the oil and season both sides with the salt and pepper. Grill for 3 to 4 minutes per side until slightly charred and cooked to medium-well (page 12).

3. Remove the tuna from the grill and transfer to a cutting board. Let rest for 5 minutes, then cut into small dice or flake with a fork. Add the tuna to the mayonnaise mixture and gently mix to combine. *The tuna salad can be made up to 8 hours in advance and kept refrigerated.*

4. Divide the tuna salad among 6 slices of the bread, top the salad with a few sprigs of watercress, then cover with the remaining 6 slices bread.

Grilled Tuna with Fennel-Tomatillo Relish

Fennel and tomatillos may seem to be an unlikely combination, but it works. Tomatillos are juicy and slightly acidic, and I love their herbal, lemony taste. The sweet fennel with its anise flavor and tart tomatillos make a crunchy and sweet relish that pairs perfectly with tuna. I like my tuna cooked medium-rare—nice and pink on the inside and crusty on the outside.

Serves 4

**BOBBY
FLAY'S
GRILLING
FOR
LIFE**

112

FENNEL-TOMATILLO RELISH
¼ cup white wine vinegar

3 tablespoons chopped fresh cilantro leaves

1 tablespoon grated lemon zest

1 teaspoon honey

¼ teaspoon kosher salt

¼ teaspoon freshly ground black pepper

½ cup olive oil

½ fennel bulb, trimmed and thinly sliced

4 tomatillos, husked, washed, and cut
   into eighths

½ medium red onion, thinly sliced

2 cloves garlic, thinly sliced

1 jalapeño chile, finely chopped

Nutritional Analysis (per serving)

Calories: **650**   Protein (gm): **54**   Carbohydrates (gm): **8**

Total Sugar (gm): **2.6**   Total Fat (gm): **43**   Saturated Fat (gm): **7**

Cholesterol (mg): **86**   Sodium (mg): **479**   Fiber (gm): **3**

Whisk together the vinegar, cilantro, zest, honey, salt, and pepper in a large bowl. Slowly drizzle in the olive oil and whisk until emulsified. Add the remaining ingredients and stir to combine. Cover and refrigerate for at least 30 minutes and up to 2 hours before serving.

GRILLED TUNA
1 tablespoon ancho chile powder
1 teaspoon ground fennel seeds
1 teaspoon kosher salt
½ teaspoon freshly ground black pepper
4 tuna steaks, 8 ounces each
4 teaspoons olive oil

1. Heat your grill to high. Combine the ancho powder, fennel, salt, and pepper in a small bowl.

2. Brush the tuna steaks with the oil and season one side of each steak with the ancho mixture. Grill spice side down until charred and crusty, about 2 minutes. Turn the fish over and continue cooking for 2 to 3 minutes for medium-rare (page 12). Remove from the grill and let rest for 5 minutes.

3. Top the tuna steaks with fennel-tomatillo relish before serving.

Grilled Tuna Burgers with Green Onion Mayonnaise and Watercress

BOBBY
FLAY'S
GRILLING
FOR
LIFE

114

A great change from beef burgers. These highly seasoned tuna burgers have a meaty texture but—surprise—they're fish! They cook quickly, so man the grill closely. Also note that I prefer these burgers to be cooked to medium and not the usual medium-rare that I want in a whole tuna steak. I think the texture of cooked diced tuna is better that way, and I want a burger that's hot all the way through.

Serves 4

GREEN ONION MAYONNAISE

½ cup mayonnaise

1 clove garlic, chopped

3 green onions, light and dark parts, chopped

2 teaspoons fresh lime juice

¼ teaspoon kosher salt

¼ teaspoon freshly ground black pepper

Combine all of the ingredients in a blender and blend until smooth. Cover and refrigerate for at least 1 hour and up to 4 hours before serving.

Nutritional Analysis (per serving with 1 tablespoon mayonnaise)

Calories: **637**   Protein (gm): **60**   Carbohydrates (gm): **27**

Total Sugar (gm): **3**   Total Fat (gm): **32**   Saturated Fat (gm): **5**

Cholesterol (mg): **91**   Sodium (mg): **657**   Fiber (gm): **3.5**

TUNA BURGERS

2 tablespoons Dijon mustard

2 tablespoons canola oil

1 tablespoon chipotle purée (page 17)

1 tablespoon fresh lime juice

1 teaspoon honey

2 green onions, light and dark parts, thinly sliced

3 tablespoons finely chopped fresh cilantro leaves

2 pounds fresh tuna steaks, finely chopped

¼ teaspoon kosher salt

¼ teaspoon freshly ground black pepper

1 small bunch watercress

4 whole grain rolls

1. Combine the mustard, oil, chipotle purée, lime juice, honey, green onions, and cilantro in a large bowl. Add the chopped tuna and gently fold together with a rubber spatula to combine. Shape the mixture with your hands into 4 round patties about 1½ inches thick. Refrigerate for at least 30 minutes and up to 2 hours; the burgers must be very cold to hold their shape when cooking.

2. Heat your grill to high.

3. Season the burgers with the salt and pepper and grill for 3 minutes on each side for medium (page 12).

4. Serve each burger topped with 1 tablespoon of the mayonnaise and several leaves of watercress sandwiched between the rolls. Serve the remaining mayonnaise on the side if desired.

Tuna au Poivre Salad
with Creamy Tarragon-Garlic Vinaigrette

BOBBY
FLAY'S
GRILLING
FOR
LIFE

116

This recipe is a take on the classic Niçoise salad, which has become a staple on menus everywhere. Now put it on your grill menu but kick it up first with black pepper and tarragon. The important Niçoise elements are here—eggs, anchovies, green beans, Niçoise olives, and tuna—just rearranged. This elegant salad is perfect for an outdoor luncheon.

Serves 4

CREAMY HERB-TARRAGON DRESSING

¼ cup white wine vinegar

4 hard-cooked egg yolks
   (keep the whites for the salad, page 118)

2 anchovy fillets

2 cloves garlic, chopped

3 tablespoons water

2 tablespoons chopped fresh tarragon leaves

1 tablespoon Dijon mustard

1 teaspoon grated lemon zest

¼ teaspoon kosher salt

¼ teaspoon freshly ground black pepper

½ cup olive oil

Nutritional Analysis (per serving)

Calories: **678**   Protein (gm): **61**   Carbohydrates (gm): **8**

Total Sugar (gm): **0**   Total Fat (gm): **44**   Saturated Fat (gm): **7**

Cholesterol (mg): **242**   Sodium (mg): **660**   Fiber (gm): **3**

Combine the vinegar, egg yolks, anchovies, garlic, water, tarragon, mustard, zest, salt, and pepper in a blender and blend until smooth. With the motor running, slowly drizzle in the oil and blend until emulsified. Cover and refrigerate for at least 1 hour and up to 2 hours before serving.

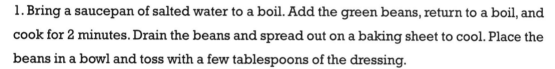

TUNA SALAD
4 ounces haricots verts or thin green beans
4 tuna steaks, 6 ounces each
2 teaspoons canola oil
1 teaspoon kosher salt
4 teaspoons coarsely ground black pepper
2 cups mesclun greens
4 hard-cooked egg whites, finely chopped
½ cup Niçoise olives, pitted

1. Bring a saucepan of salted water to a boil. Add the green beans, return to a boil, and cook for 2 minutes. Drain the beans and spread out on a baking sheet to cool. Place the beans in a bowl and toss with a few tablespoons of the dressing.

2. Heat your grill to high.

3. Brush the tuna with the oil and season both sides with the salt. Season each steak on one side only with 1 teaspoon black pepper. Place the tuna pepper side down on the grill and grill until a crust has formed, 2 to 3 minutes. Turn the fish over and continue cooking for 1 to 2 minutes for medium-rare (page 12). Remove to a cutting board and let rest for 5 minutes before cutting into ¼-inch-thick slices.

4. Place the mesclun greens in a large bowl and toss with a few tablespoons of the dressing. Arrange the mesclun on a large platter. Arrange the sliced tuna on the perimeter of the platter. Place the green beans in the center and sprinkle the beans with the egg whites. Drizzle the remaining dressing over the tuna and greens and garnish with the olives.

BOBBY
FLAY'S
GRILLING
FOR
LIFE

118

HARD-COOKED EGGS

Place eggs in a medium saucepan, cover with cold water, and bring to a boil over high heat. Cover, remove from the heat, and let stand for 15 minutes. Drain the eggs, cover with cold water and let sit for another 5 minutes. Drain and use immediately or cover and refrigerate for up to 3 days.

POULTRY

Grilled Chicken Cutlets with Lemon and Black Pepper and Arugula-Tomato Salad

Like chicken Milanese, the classic Italian batter-fried chicken dish, this is practically a one-plate meal. I love the idea of a cold, crisp salad served over a hot breast of chicken but, of course, I had to adapt that egg-and-flour-battered breast for the grill. This fresh version is light and flavorful, and I love the way the peppery arugula brings out the black pepper in the marinade. The chicken should be pounded thin with a meat mallet (like a chicken minute steak).

Serves 4

¼ cup fresh lemon juice

¼ cup plus 2 tablespoons olive oil

1 small shallot, chopped

½ teaspoon coarsely ground fresh black pepper

4 boneless, skinless chicken breasts, 8 ounces each

½ teaspoon kosher salt

8 ounces arugula

2 ripe beefsteak tomatoes, diced

1 small red onion, halved and thinly sliced

2 tablespoons red wine vinegar

Nutritional Analysis (per serving)

Calories: **441**   Protein (gm): **55**   Carbohydrates (gm): **9**

Total Sugar (gm): **5**   Total Fat (gm): **20**   Saturated Fat (gm): **3**

Cholesterol (mg): **131**   Sodium (mg): **237**   Fiber (gm): **2**

1. Whisk together the lemon juice, ¼ cup of the olive oil, the shallot, and ¼ teaspoon of the black pepper in a large baking dish.

2. Pound each chicken breast ⅛ inch thick between 2 sheets of wax paper or plastic wrap with a rolling pin or meat mallet. Add the chicken to the baking dish, turn to coat, cover, and marinate in the refrigerator for at least 1 hour and up to 4 hours.

3. Heat your grill to high.

4. Remove the chicken from the marinade and season both sides with ¼ teaspoon of the salt. Grill for 2 to 3 minutes per side until golden brown and just cooked through.

5. While the chicken is grilling, combine the arugula, tomatoes, and onion in a large bowl. Toss with the vinegar and remaining 2 tablespoons oil, then season with the remaining ¼ teaspoon salt and ¼ teaspoon pepper.

6. Place each chicken cutlet on a large plate and top with the arugula-tomato salad.

Grilled Chicken Breasts
with Fontina and Prosciutto
with Sage-Orange Vinaigrette

**BOBBY
FLAY'S
GRILLING
FOR
LIFE**

122

Fontina cheese, sage, and prosciutto are standard Italian ingredients found in many recipes throughout northern Italy, one of the most famous being chicken saltimbocca. I have lightened up that classic dish for the grill. The vinaigrette, heady with sage and fresh orange zest, guarantees that you won't miss the sautéed standard one bit.

Serves 4

SAGE-ORANGE VINAIGRETTE

¼ **cup white wine vinegar**

3 **tablespoons chopped fresh sage leaves**

1 **clove garlic, chopped**

2 **teaspoons grated orange zest**

¼ **teaspoon kosher salt**

¼ **teaspoon freshly ground black pepper**

½ **cup olive oil**

Combine the vinegar, sage, garlic, orange zest, salt, and pepper in a blender and blend until smooth. With the motor running, slowly drizzle in the oil and blend until emulsified.

Nutritional Analysis (per serving)

Calories: **576**   Protein (gm): **59**   Carbohydrates (gm): **2**

Total Sugar (gm): **0**   Total Fat (gm): **35**   Saturated Fat (gm): **6.7**

Cholesterol (mg): **158**   Sodium (mg): **656**   Fiber (gm): **0**

STUFFED CHICKEN BREASTS

4 boneless, skinless chicken breasts, 8 ounces each

4 slices prosciutto (2 ounces)

2 ounces fontina cheese, coarsely grated

4 fresh sage leaves

About 12 wooden toothpicks, soaked in water for 5 minutes

2 tablespoons olive oil

½ teaspoon kosher salt

½ teaspoon freshly ground black pepper

Grilled orange wedges (page 26)

1. Heat your grill to high.

2. Pound each chicken breast ⅛ inch thick between 2 sheets of wax paper or plastic wrap with a rolling pin or meat mallet. Lay the chicken breasts out on a flat surface and top each breast with 1 slice prosciutto, some grated cheese, and 1 sage leaf. Roll each breast up crosswise and secure with a few toothpicks by threading them through the seam side of each breast.

3. Brush the breasts with the olive oil and season with salt and pepper. Grill for 6 to 8 minutes, turning as needed, until golden brown on all sides and cooked through (page 12).

4. Remove the breasts to a platter and drizzle each breast with 2 tablespoons of the sage-orange vinaigrette. Let rest for 5 minutes. Garnish with grilled orange wedges. Serve the remaining vinaigrette on the side if desired.

Grilled Chicken Breasts Stuffed with Goat Cheese with Green Chile–Cilantro Sauce

BOBBY
FLAY'S
GRILLING
FOR
LIFE

124

This tasty chicken dish packs a great surprise with its luscious goat cheese, olive, and red pepper filling. Green chiles and goat cheese are made for each other, making this sauce the perfect complement for the chicken. I like to serve this incredibly versatile sauce with everything from grilled vegetables to steak and even eggs for breakfast.

Serves 4

GREEN CHILE–CILANTRO SAUCE

2 poblano chiles, grilled (page 25), peeled, and chopped

¼ cup coarsely chopped red onion

2 cloves garlic, chopped

3 tablespoons fresh lime juice

2 tablespoons water

2 teaspoons grated lime zest

2 teaspoons honey

½ teaspoon kosher salt

¼ teaspoon freshly ground black pepper

½ cup olive oil

¼ cup fresh cilantro leaves

Nutritional Analysis (per serving with 2 tablespoons sauce)

Calories: **567** Protein (gm): **59** Carbohydrates (gm): **9**

Total Sugar (gm): **4** Total Fat (gm): **32** Saturated Fat (gm): **8**

Cholesterol (mg): **144** Sodium (mg): **517** Fiber (gm): **1.5**

Combine the poblanos, onion, garlic, lime juice, water, zest, honey, salt, and pepper in a blender and blend until smooth. While the motor is running, slowly drizzle in the oil and blend until emulsified. Add the cilantro and blend until smooth. If the sauce appears too thick, thin it by adding a few tablespoons of cold water. *The sauce can be made up to 1 day in advance, covered, and kept refrigerated.*

STUFFED CHICKEN BREASTS

4 ounces soft goat cheese
¼ cup chopped pitted Niçoise olives
1 red bell pepper, grilled (page 25), peeled,
    seeded, and chopped
1 tablespoon chopped fresh thyme leaves
1 teaspoon freshly ground black pepper
4 boneless, skinless chicken breasts, 8 ounces each
About 12 wooden toothpicks, soaked in water
    for 5 minutes
4 teaspoons olive oil
½ teaspoon kosher salt

1. Heat your grill to high.

2. Mix together the goat cheese, olives, red pepper, and thyme in a small bowl and season with ¼ teaspoon of the pepper.

3. Pound each chicken breast ⅛ inch thick between 2 sheets of wax paper or plastic wrap with a rolling pin or meat mallet. Spread the goat cheese mixture evenly over the breasts and roll up each breast crosswise. Secure with a few toothpicks by threading them through the seam side of each breast. Brush the breasts with the olive oil and season with the salt and remaining ¾ teaspoon pepper.

4. Grill the chicken for 6 to 8 minutes, turning as needed, until golden brown on all sides and cooked through (page 12).

5. Remove the breasts to a platter and drizzle each breast with 2 tablespoons of the chile-cilantro sauce. Let rest for 5 minutes. Serve the remaining sauce on the side if desired.

Chinese Chicken Salad
with Red Chile–Peanut Dressing

**BOBBY
FLAY'S
GRILLING
FOR
LIFE**

126

Chinese chicken salads have been popular since Wolfgang Puck put his version on the culinary map in the early 1980s. This is my favorite version. The dressing has heat and smokiness from the chipotles and a deep nuttiness from both the peanut butter (be sure to use smooth!) and the toasted sesame oil.

Serves 6

RED CHILE–PEANUT DRESSING

3 tablespoons low-sodium soy sauce

3 tablespoons rice vinegar

¼ cup low-sodium chicken stock

3 tablespoons smooth natural peanut butter

1 tablespoon light brown sugar

1 tablespoon grated fresh ginger

1 tablespoon chipotle purée (page 17)

2 teaspoons toasted sesame oil

¼ teaspoon freshly ground black pepper

Whisk together all of the ingredients in a medium bowl. *The dressing will keep covered in the refrigerator for up to 2 days.*

Nutritional Analysis (per serving)

Calories: **438**   Protein (gm): **61**   Carbohydrates (gm): **19**

Total Sugar (gm): **7**   Total Fat (gm): **14**   Saturated Fat (gm): **2**

Cholesterol (mg): **132**   Sodium (mg): **734**   Fiber (gm): **7**

CHICKEN SALAD

½ head Napa cabbage

½ head romaine lettuce

2 medium carrots, peeled

4 ounces snow peas (about 1 cup),
    trimmed

¼ cup coarsely chopped fresh
    cilantro leaves

¼ cup thinly sliced green onions,
    light and dark parts

4 boneless, skinless chicken breasts,
    8 ounces each

1 tablespoon canola oil

1 teaspoon kosher salt

½ teaspoon freshly ground black pepper

¼ cup chopped roasted peanuts

Grilled lime wedges (page 26)

1. Finely slice the cabbage and romaine lettuce with a large, sharp knife and place in a large bowl. Shred the carrots on the large holes of a box grater and add to the cabbage mixture. Add the snow peas, cilantro, and green onions and set aside for the moment.

2. Heat your grill to high.

3. Brush each chicken breast on both sides with the oil and season with the salt and pepper. Grill for 4 minutes on each side until slightly charred and just cooked through (page 12). Remove from the grill, transfer to a cutting board, and let rest for 5 minutes. Shred the chicken: Hold the edge of a breast with a pair of tongs, rest the chicken on the cutting board, and use a fork to pull apart the meat.

4. Add the dressing to the cabbage mixture and toss well to combine. Transfer the mixture to a large platter, top with the shredded chicken and chopped peanuts, and garnish with grilled lime wedges.

Spanish-Spiced Chicken with Mustard–Green Onion Sauce

It's amazing the way these spices come together to create one big flavor. Not only does this rub have dynamic taste, but it also creates a fantastic contrast of textures. This dish has become a favorite at my restaurant Bolo. Feel free to experiment with the spice rub. This is what works best according to my taste, but you might like to change the proportions or try adding hot or smoked paprika for a more piquant flavor.

Serves 4

MUSTARD–GREEN ONION SAUCE

¼ cup white wine vinegar

2 tablespoons Dijon mustard

⅓ cup olive oil

¼ teaspoon kosher salt

¼ teaspoon freshly ground
    black pepper

¼ cup thinly sliced green onions,
    light and dark parts

2 tablespoons finely chopped fresh
    flat-leaf parsley leaves

Nutritional Analysis (per serving with 2 tablespoons sauce)

Calories: **496**   Protein (gm): **55**   Carbohydrates (gm): **7**

Total Sugar (gm): **1**   Total Fat (gm): **27**   Saturated Fat (gm): **4**

Cholesterol (mg): **132**   Sodium (mg): **882**   Fiber (gm): **3**

Whisk together the vinegar and mustard in a large bowl. Drizzle in the oil and whisk to emulsify. Season with the salt and pepper, then stir in the green onions and parsley.

SPANISH SPICE RUB

3 tablespoons Spanish paprika

1 tablespoon ground cumin seeds

1 tablespoon ground mustard seeds

2 teaspoons ground fennel seeds

2 teaspoons kosher salt

2 teaspoons coarsely ground black pepper

Whisk together all of the ingredients in a bowl.

CHICKEN

4 bone-in skinless chicken breasts, 8 ounces each

4 teaspoons olive oil

Chopped fresh flat-leaf parsley leaves

---

1. Heat your grill to medium.

2. Rub each chicken breast on the top side with the rub, drizzle with the oil, and place rub side down on the grill. Grill for 3 to 4 minutes until slightly charred and a crust has formed. Turn the breasts over, close the cover, and continue cooking for 5 to 6 minutes until just cooked through (page 12). Remove to a cutting board and let rest for 5 minutes.

3. Place the chicken breasts on a platter and drizzle 2 tablespoons of the sauce over each breast. Garnish with chopped parsley, and serve the remaining sauce on the side if desired.

Grilled Chicken Tenders with Spicy Chipotle Sauce and Blue Cheese–Yogurt Sauce

Who doesn't love sitting down to a cold beer and a basket of Buffalo chicken wings? I've taken that American bar food staple and mixed it up just enough to make things interesting. Smoked jalapeños round out the hot sauce with their fiery flavor, and thick Greek yogurt replaces the traditional mayonnaise and sour cream dipping sauce. I've lightened the dish even further by replacing the wings with lean chicken tenders, which are grilled, not deep fried. You can't get rid of the blue cheese, though.

Serves 6

BLUE CHEESE-YOGURT SAUCE

1 cup nonfat Greek yogurt

¼ cup crumbled blue cheese

2 tablespoons finely grated red onion

2 tablespoons finely chopped fresh cilantro leaves

¼ teaspoon kosher salt

¼ teaspoon freshly ground black pepper

Combine all of the ingredients in a bowl. Cover and refrigerate for at least 30 minutes and up to 8 hours before serving.

Nutritional Analysis (per serving with 2 tablespoons hot sauce)

Calories: **335**	Protein (gm): **39**	Carbohydrates (gm): **8**
Total Sugar (gm): **6**	Total Fat (gm): **15**	Saturated Fat (gm): **4**
Cholesterol (mg): **100**	Sodium (mg): **446**	Fiber (gm): **.5**

GRILLED CHICKEN TENDERS

2 pounds chicken tenders

1 tablespoon olive oil

$\frac{1}{2}$ teaspoon salt

$\frac{1}{2}$ teaspoon freshly ground black pepper

---

1. Heat your grill to high.

2. Toss the chicken tenders with the oil, salt, and pepper. Grill until golden brown on both sides and just cooked through (page 12), about 3 minutes per side. Remove the tenders from the grill and place in a large bowl while you prepare the spicy chipotle sauce. Lower the heat of the grill to medium.

SPICY CHIPOTLE SAUCE

$1\frac{1}{2}$ cups red wine vinegar

3 tablespoons vegetable oil

2 to 3 tablespoons chipotle purée

(depending on how spicy you like it; page 17)

2 tablespoons honey

2 tablespoons ancho chile powder

1 tablespoon ground New Mexico chile powder

3 tablespoons Dijon mustard

3 tablespoons unsalted butter, cold, cut into pieces

---

1. Bring the vinegar, oil, chipotle purée, honey, and both chile powders to a simmer in a medium saucepan over medium heat on the grill. Remove the mixture from the heat and whisk in the mustard and butter.

2. Pour half of the chipotle sauce over the tenders and toss well to combine. Divide the tenders and blue cheese sauce among 6 plates. Serve the remaining chipotle sauce on the side if desired.

Grilled Turkey Burgers with Monterey Jack, Poblano Pickle Relish, and Avocado Mayonnaise

BOBBY
FLAY'S
GRILLING
FOR
LIFE

132

Turkey burgers have become *the* alternative to hamburgers. Ground turkey is a great choice because of its low fat content, but that often means the burgers are dry and bland. Not these! The slightly spicy pickle relish and the cooling avocado mayonnaise infuse the burgers with flavor through and through.

Serves 4

POBLANO PICKLE RELISH

2 poblano chiles, grilled (page 25), peeled, seeded, and finely chopped

1 large or 2 medium dill pickles, finely chopped

1 small red onion, finely chopped

¼ cup fresh lime juice

1 teaspoon honey

¼ teaspoon salt

2 tablespoons finely chopped fresh cilantro leaves

¼ teaspoon freshly ground black pepper

Combine all of the ingredients in a medium bowl. Cover and let sit at room temperature for at least 30 minutes and up to 4 hours before serving.

Nutritional Analysis (per serving with 1 tablespoon avocado mayonnaise)

Calories: **495**   Protein (gm): **57**   Carbohydrates (gm): **12**

Total Sugar (gm): **3.8**   Total Fat (gm): **22**   Saturated Fat (gm): **5.7**

Cholesterol (mg): **106**   Sodium (mg): **1,025**   Fiber (gm): **2.2**

AVOCADO MAYONNAISE
½ ripe Hass avocado, peeled and chopped

¼ cup mayonnaise

1 tablespoon fresh lime juice

2 cloves garlic, chopped

½ teaspoon ground cumin

¼ teaspoon kosher salt

¼ teaspoon freshly ground black pepper

Place all of the ingredients in a food processor and process until smooth.

TURKEY BURGERS
1½ pounds ground turkey, 99% lean

2 tablespoons canola oil

½ teaspoon kosher salt

½ teaspoon freshly ground black pepper

4 slices Monterey Jack cheese, ½ ounce each

1. Heat your grill to high.

2. Shape the ground turkey with your hands into 4 round patties about 1½ inches thick. Brush each burger on both sides with the oil and season with the salt and pepper. Grill until slightly charred on both sides and cooked completely through (page 12), about 4 minutes per side. Place a slice of cheese on each burger, close the lid of the grill, and cook for 1 minute longer to melt the cheese. Transfer to a cutting board and let rest for 5 minutes.

3. Top each burger with 1 tablespoon of the avocado mayonnaise and a few table-spoons of the relish. Serve the remaining avocado mayonnaise on the side if desired.

Grilled Turkey Cutlets with Sage-Lemon Pesto

BOBBY
FLAY'S
GRILLING
FOR
LIFE

134

On its own, turkey always needs additional moisture and flavor. The marinade infuses the meat with both, and the garlicky, herbaceous pesto puts these cutlets over the top taste-wise. Turkey with sage—it's a no-brainer, and not just a combination you eat at Thanksgiving.

Serves 4

SAGE-LEMON PESTO
¼ **cup fresh sage leaves**
¼ **cup fresh flat-leaf parsley leaves**
1 **clove garlic, smashed**
2 **tablespoons pine nuts**
⅓ **cup olive oil**
3 **tablespoons grated Parmesan cheese**
¼ **teaspoon kosher salt**
¼ **teaspoons freshly ground black pepper**

Combine the sage, parsley, garlic, and pine nuts in a food processor or blender and process until coarsely chopped. With the motor running, slowly drizzle in the oil and

Nutritional Analysis (per serving)

Calories: **599**   Protein (gm): **59**   Carbohydrates (gm): **5**

Total Sugar (gm): **0**   Total Fat (gm): **37**   Saturated Fat (gm): **5**

Cholesterol (mg): **144**   Sodium (mg): **522**   Fiber (gm): **0**

process until emulsified. Add the cheese, salt, and pepper and process 3 to 4 seconds longer. *The pesto can be made up to 2 days in advance, covered, and refrigerated.*

GRILLED TURKEY CUTLETS

¼ cup olive oil
2 tablespoons fresh lemon juice
1 teaspoon grated lemon zest
2 cloves garlic, finely chopped
1 teaspoon coriander seeds
4 turkey breast cutlets, 8 ounces each
1 teaspoon kosher salt
1 teaspoon freshly ground black pepper

---

1. Whisk together the oil, lemon juice, zest, garlic, and coriander seeds in a shallow baking dish. Add the cutlets and turn to coat. Cover and let marinate in the refrigerator for at least 1 hour and up to 4 hours.

2. Heat your grill to high.

3. Remove the cutlets from the marinade and season on both sides with the salt and pepper. Grill the cutlets for 3 to 4 minutes on each side until golden brown and just cooked through (page 12). Remove from the grill and let rest for 5 minutes.

4. Top each turkey cutlet with pesto before serving.

Bricked Rosemary Chicken with Lemon

A Tuscan classic! The brick technique ensures a crisp exterior with a moist and juicy interior. The sprinkling of lemon zest and herbs keeps it tasting fresh. Butterflying the chicken is an easy procedure with the right knife or pair of kitchen shears (see box), but you can always ask a butcher to do it for you.

Serves 6

BOBBY
FLAY'S
GRILLING
FOR
LIFE

136

¼ **cup olive oil**

¼ **cup fresh lemon juice**

1 tablespoon plus 2 teaspoons
      finely grated lemon zest

10 cloves garlic, finely chopped

4 tablespoons chopped fresh rosemary leaves

Two chickens, about 3 pounds each,
      skin removed, butterflied
      (see box, page 137)

3 tablespoons finely chopped flat-leaf
      parsley leaves

1¼ **teaspoons kosher salt**

1¼ **teaspoons freshly ground black pepper**

Grilled lemon wedges (page 26)

Nutritional Analysis (per serving)

Calories: **417**   Protein (gm): **65**   Carbohydrates (gm): **3**

Total Sugar (gm): **0**   Total Fat (gm): **14**   Saturated Fat (gm): **3**

Cholesterol (mg): **206**   Sodium (mg): **474**   Fiber (gm): **0**

1. Whisk together the oil, lemon juice, 1 tablespoon of the zest, 6 cloves of the garlic, and 3 tablespoons of the rosemary in a large baking dish. Add the chickens and turn to coat. Cover and marinate in the refrigerator for at least 1 hour and up to 8 hours.

2. Combine the parsley with the remaining 2 teaspoons lemon zest, 4 cloves garlic, 1 tablespoon rosemary, ¼ teaspoon of the salt, and ¼ teaspoon of the pepper in a small bowl and set aside.

3. Heat your grill to medium. Wrap 4 bricks in aluminum foil and set aside.

4. Remove the chickens from the marinade, shaking off the excess, and season both sides with the remaining 1 teaspoon salt and 1 teaspoon pepper. Place the chickens breast side down on the grill and place 2 bricks on top of each chicken. Grill the chickens for 8 to 10 minutes, turn the chickens over, and replace the bricks. Close the cover and continue cooking for 8 to 10 minutes until cooked through (page 12).

5. Transfer the chickens to a cutting board and let rest for 10 minutes. Cut into quarters and sprinkle with the fresh lemon mixture. Serve with grilled lemon wedges.

TO BUTTERFLY CHICKEN

Place the chicken breast side down on a cutting board and cut along each side of the backbone using kitchen shears or a sharp knife. Remove the backbone and discard. Turn the chicken breast side up and pull out each side where the backbone was removed. Using the heel of your hand to press down on the breast, break the breastbone to flatten the chicken.

Balsamic-Thyme-Glazed Duck Breasts

BOBBY
FLAY'S
GRILLING
FOR
LIFE

138

For some reason, people think of duck only as restaurant fare. It shouldn't be. Duck is available in most grocery stores today and online at www.dartagnan.com. A skinless duck breast can be easier to grill than a piece of chicken. Here the balsamic vinegar adds tartness and sweetness to the rich-tasting duck. Be sure to cook them medium-rare to medium—it's okay if they are a little pink in the middle.

Serves 4

½ cup plus 2 tablespoons balsamic vinegar

1 tablespoon olive oil

2 cloves garlic, chopped

1 tablespoon chopped fresh thyme leaves

2 teaspoons coarsely ground black pepper

4 boneless, skinless duck breasts,
    8 ounces each

1 teaspoon salt

1. Whisk together ½ cup of the vinegar, the oil, garlic, thyme, and pepper in a shallow baking dish. Add the duck breasts and turn to coat. Cover the dish and refrigerate for at least 1 hour and up to 8 hours.

2. Heat your grill to high.

Nutritional Analysis (per serving)

Calories: **367**   Protein (gm): **45**   Carbohydrates (gm): **12.5**

Total Sugar (gm): **11**   Total Fat (gm): **13**   Saturated Fat (gm): **3**

Cholesterol (mg): **175**   Sodium (mg): **417**   Fiber (gm): **0**

3. Remove the duck from the marinade, season with the salt, and grill the breasts for 3 to 4 minutes per side until slightly charred and cooked to medium-rare (page 12). Transfer to a cutting board and let rest for 5 minutes.

4. Cut the duck into ½-inch-thick slices and drizzle the breasts with the remaining 2 tablespoons vinegar before serving.

Grilled Duck Breast
with Black Pepper–Sweet Mustard Sauce

BOBBY
FLAY'S
GRILLING
FOR
LIFE

140

Removing the skin makes the duck breast low in fat. Treat these like any other meat and be sure not to overcook them. I think that they taste best cooked medium-rare to medium. This is a great entrée for someone looking for a quick and easy, low-calorie dinner.

Serves 4

BLACK PEPPER–SWEET MUSTARD SAUCE

¼ cup Dijon mustard

2 tablespoons whole grain mustard

1 tablespoon water

2 teaspoons honey

1 teaspoon coarsely ground
    black pepper

1 teaspoon finely chopped fresh
    thyme leaves

Whisk together all of the ingredients in a small bowl.

Nutritional Analysis (per serving)

Calories: **307**   Protein (gm): **56**   Carbohydrates (gm): **7**

Total Sugar (gm): **3**   Total Fat (gm): **6**   Saturated Fat (gm): **1**

Cholesterol (mg): **131**   Sodium (mg): **890**   Fiber (gm): **0**

GRILLED DUCK BREASTS

**4 boneless, skinless duck breasts,
  8 ounces each**

2 teaspoons canola oil

2 teaspoons ground coriander

1 teaspoon kosher salt

1. Heat your grill to high.

2. Brush the duck breasts with the oil and season with the coriander and salt. Grill the breasts for 3 to 4 minutes per side until slightly charred and cooked to medium-rare (page 12). Transfer to a cutting board and let rest for 5 minutes.

3. Cut each breast into ½-inch-thick slices and drizzle with the sauce before serving.

PORK, BEEF, AND LAMB

Pork Tenderloin Crusted with Green Onion, Jalapeño, and Ginger

BOBBY
FLAY'S
GRILLING
FOR
LIFE

144

I always want lots of flavor when I grill, and I know that this green onion, jalapeño, and ginger marinade provides it. This thick marinade—which could really be called a wet rub—allows you to grill the pork with a liberal amount of the marinade intact. Not only will it lend phenomenal flavor, but it also gives the pork great texture too.

Serves 4

6 green onions, light and dark parts,
    halved crosswise
2 jalapeño chiles, stemmed and halved
1 (2-inch) piece fresh ginger, peeled
½ cup canola oil
¼ cup fresh lime juice
1 tablespoon low-sodium soy sauce
2 teaspoons toasted sesame oil
2 teaspoons grated lime zest
¼ teaspoon freshly ground black pepper
2 pounds pork tenderloin

Nutritional Analysis (per serving)

Calories: **563**   Protein (gm): **72**   Carbohydrates (gm): **3**

Total Sugar (gm): **1**   Total Fat (gm): **27**   Saturated Fat (gm): **5**

Cholesterol (mg): **221**   Sodium (mg): **244**   Fiber (gm): **1**

1. Combine the green onions, jalapeños, and ginger in a food processor and process until coarsely ground. (Alternatively, coarsely chop the ingredients with a sharp knife.) Scrape the mixture into a bowl and stir in all of the remaining ingredients except the pork.

2. Place the pork tenderloins in a baking dish, add half of the marinade, and turn to coat the pork. Cover and refrigerate for at least 30 minutes and up to 4 hours. Cover and reserve the remaining marinade at room temperature.

3. Heat your grill to high.

4. Remove the pork from the marinade. Grill until crusty and charred on both sides and cooked to medium-well (page 12), 4 to 5 minutes per side. Transfer to a cutting board and let rest for 5 minutes.

5. Cut the pork into ½-inch-thick slices. Drizzle the sliced pork with the reserved marinade before serving.

Grilled Fennel-Spiced Pork Chops with Sage-Lemon Vinaigrette

BOBBY
FLAY'S
GRILLING
FOR
LIFE

146

Don't tell your friends or family what is on this pork. Let them try to place that sweet anise flavor on their own. Fennel seed is an underused spice that really is fantastic. It's a great way to create flavor without adding any extra calories. The sage and lemon vinaigrette would also work well on grilled chicken and turkey.

Serves 4

SAGE-LEMON VINAIGRETTE

3 tablespoons chopped fresh sage leaves

¼ cup fresh lemon juice

2 teaspoons grated lemon zest

½ shallot, coarsely chopped

1 teaspoon honey

¼ teaspoon kosher salt

¼ teaspoon freshly ground black pepper

⅓ cup olive oil

Combine the sage, lemon juice, zest, shallot, honey, salt, and pepper in a blender and blend until smooth. With the motor running, slowly drizzle in the oil and blend until emulsified.

Nutritional Analysis (per serving with 2 tablespoons vinaigrette)

Calories: **539**   Protein (gm): **51**   Carbohydrates (gm): **6**

Total Sugar (gm): **1**   Total Fat (gm): **34**   Saturated Fat (gm): **6.6**

Cholesterol (mg): **143**   Sodium (mg): **761**   Fiber (gm): **2**

FENNEL-SPICED PORK CHOPS

2 tablespoons fennel seeds

2 teaspoons kosher salt

2 teaspoons whole black peppercorns

4 thick center-cut boneless pork chops,
    8 ounces each

1 tablespoon canola oil

1. Heat your grill to medium-high. Place the fennel seeds, salt, and peppercorns in a coffee or spice mill and process until finely ground. Alternatively, combine the spices on a cutting board and crush them with the bottom of a heavy pot.

2. Brush the pork chops with the oil and season on both sides with the fennel mixture. Grill the chops until slightly charred on both sides and cooked to medium-well (page 12), 4 to 5 minutes per side.

3. Transfer the chops to a plate and immediately drizzle each chop with 2 tablespoons of the sage-lemon vinaigrette. Let the chops rest for 5 minutes before serving. Serve the remaining vinaigrette on the side if desired.

Pork Satay with Red Chile–Peanut Sauce and Napa Cabbage–Green Onion Slaw

Pork tenderloin is a great cut for this dish for it has very little fat and cooks quickly on the grill. Make sure that you use unsweetened coconut milk and natural peanut butter—the sauce is savory, not sweet.

Serves 6

PORK MARINADE

¼ cup low-sodium soy sauce

2 tablespoons peanut oil

2 tablespoons finely chopped fresh ginger

4 cloves garlic, finely chopped

1 teaspoon coarsely ground black pepper

2 pounds pork tenderloin

Whisk together the soy sauce, peanut oil, ginger, garlic, and pepper in a medium bowl. Cut the tenderloin lengthwise in half, then cut the halves lengthwise in half again. Slice crosswise to make 24 equal pieces. Add the cubed pork and toss to combine. Cover and marinate in the refrigerator for at least 1 hour and up to 4 hours.

Nutritional Analysis (per serving with 2 tablespoons sauce)

Calories: **400**	Protein (gm): **38**	Carbohydrates (gm): **9**
Total Sugar (gm): **2**	Total Fat (gm): **23**	Saturated Fat (gm): **5**
Cholesterol (mg): **98**	Sodium (mg): **651**	Fiber (gm): **3**

NAPA CABBAGE–GREEN ONION SLAW

¼ cup rice vinegar

2 teaspoons low-sodium soy sauce

2 teaspoons toasted sesame oil

1 small head Napa cabbage, finely shredded

4 green onions, light and dark parts, thinly sliced

Whisk together the vinegar, soy sauce, and sesame oil in a medium bowl. Add the cabbage and green onions and toss to combine. Let sit at room temperature for 30 minutes and up to 1 hour before serving.

RED CHILE–PEANUT SAUCE

2 tablespoons peanut oil

1 shallot, coarsely chopped

2 tablespoons ancho chile powder

½ cup unsweetened light coconut milk

3 tablespoons low-sodium soy sauce

¼ cup natural smooth peanut butter

2 tablespoons fresh lime juice

¼ teaspoon kosher salt

¼ teaspoon freshly ground black pepper

1. Heat the oil in a small saucepan over medium heat. Add the shallot and cook, stirring occasionally, until soft, about 2 minutes. Add the ancho powder and cook for 1 minute. Add the coconut milk and soy sauce and bring to a simmer.

2. Transfer the mixture to a food processor or blender, add the peanut butter and lime juice, and process until combined. If the mixture appears too thick, begin adding water a few tablespoons at a time until the sauce has a pourable consistency. Season with the salt and pepper. Cover and keep warm.

TO GRILL

Twelve 6-inch wooden skewers, soaked in water for 30 minutes

$\frac{1}{4}$ cup chopped roasted peanuts

$\frac{1}{4}$ cup chopped pistachios

2 tablespoons finely chopped fresh flat-leaf parsley leaves

$\frac{1}{4}$ teaspoon freshly ground black pepper

1. Heat your grill to high.

2. Remove the pork from the marinade and spear 2 pieces of pork onto each skewer, keeping them together at one end of the skewer. (This will make the grilled skewer easier to hold and eat.)

3. Grill the pork, turning as needed, for 4 to 6 minutes until cooked to medium-well (page 12). Remove the skewers from the grill and let rest for 5 minutes.

4. While the pork is resting, combine the peanuts, pistachios, parsley, and pepper in a small bowl.

5. Arrange the cabbage slaw on a platter and lay the skewers on top. Drizzle 1 tablespoon peanut sauce over each skewer and sprinkle with the nut mixture. Serve the remaining sauce on the side if desired.

Espresso-Rubbed BBQ Ribs
with Mustard-Vinegar Basting Sauce

Okay, so ribs on the grill don't happen in a matter of minutes, but these are worth it. The spice rub lends flavor and creates a crust, while the baste keeps the ribs juicy. I fell in love with mustard-based BBQ sauces on my trips to the Carolinas. This sauce is perfect for those who are looking to avoid sugary sweet BBQ sauce and it works well with chicken too.

Serves 8

ESPRESSO RUB

¼ cup finely ground espresso beans

¼ cup ancho chile powder

2 tablespoons Spanish paprika

2 tablespoons dark brown sugar

1 tablespoon dry mustard

2 teaspoons kosher salt

1 tablespoon freshly ground black pepper

1 tablespoon ground cumin

1 tablespoon dried oregano

2 teaspoons ground ginger

2 teaspoons cayenne

Nutritional Analysis (per serving)

Calories: **689**   Protein (gm): **70**   Carbohydrates (gm): **16**

Total Sugar (gm): **6**   Total Fat (gm): **38**   Saturated Fat (gm): **10**

Cholesterol (mg): **217**   Sodium (mg): **709**   Fiber (gm): **4**

Combine all of the ingredients in a bowl. *The rub can be stored in a jar or another container with a tight-fitting lid in a cool, dark place for up to 1 month.*

MUSTARD-VINEGAR BASTE

3 tablespoons olive oil

1 medium Spanish onion, finely chopped

2 cloves garlic, finely chopped

1½ cups cider vinegar

½ cup water

2 tablespoons sugar

2 teaspoons mustard seeds

2 teaspoons coriander seeds

¼ cup Dijon mustard

2 tablespoons dry mustard

1 tablespoon Worcestershire sauce

Heat the oil in a medium saucepan over medium heat. Add the onion and garlic and cook, stirring occasionally, until soft, 3 to 4 minutes. Add the vinegar, water, sugar, and mustard and coriander seeds and bring to a simmer. Cook for 5 minutes, then remove from the heat. Whisk in the Dijon, dry mustard, and Worcestershire. Let cool to room temperature. *The sauce can be made up to 1 day in advance. Bring to room temperature before serving.*

RIBS

2 racks pork ribs, 3 pounds each

2 tablespoons canola oil

¼ cup thinly sliced green onions,
    light and dark parts

1. Heat your grill to medium.

2. Brush the ribs on both sides with the oil and rub with the espresso rub. Grill the ribs with the cover closed until tender, 2 to 2½ hours. Begin brushing with the mustard baste after 1 hour of grilling and continue to baste every 10 minutes thereafter. (*If using a charcoal grill:* After 1 hour, add about 2 dozen hot coals to maintain the heat.)

3. When the ribs are tender, remove from the grill, transfer to a cutting board, and brush with more of the baste. Cut into single ribs, place on a large platter, and garnish with the green onions.

Garlic-Mustard-Grilled Beef Skewers

Mustard is one of my favorite condiments. I like to use it for dressings, sauces, and, in this case, a glaze. Be sure to leave the skewers on the grill long enough to get the beef nice and crusty on both sides. This means you have to be patient, and remember: Don't turn them often.

Serves 6

**BOBBY
FLAY'S
GRILLING
FOR
LIFE**

154

GARLIC-MUSTARD GLAZE

¼ **cup whole grain mustard**

2 **tablespoons Dijon mustard**

4 **cloves garlic, finely chopped**

2 **tablespoons white wine vinegar**

1 **tablespoon low-sodium soy sauce**

1 **tablespoon honey**

1 **tablespoon finely chopped fresh
    rosemary leaves**

2 **teaspoons Spanish paprika**

¼ **teaspoon kosher salt**

¼ **teaspoon freshly ground black pepper**

Whisk together all of the ingredients in a small bowl, cover, and let sit at room temperature for at least 30 minutes and up to 4 hours before using.

Nutritional Analysis (per serving)

Calories: **406**   Protein (gm): **31**   Carbohydrates (gm): **5**

Total Sugar (gm): **3**   Total Fat (gm): **27**   Saturated Fat (gm): **11**

Cholesterol (mg): **98**   Sodium (mg): **456**   Fiber (gm): **0**

GRILLED BEEF SKEWERS

2 pounds beef tenderloin

Twelve 6-inch wooden skewers, soaked in cold water for 30 minutes

1. Heat your grill to high.

2. Cut the tenderloin lengthwise in half, then cut the halves lengthwise in half again. Slice crosswise to make 24 equal pieces. Skewer 2 pieces of beef onto each skewer, keeping them together at one end of the skewer. (This will make the grilled skewer easier to hold and eat.) Place the skewers in a baking dish or on a baking sheet, pour half of the glaze over the meat, and turn to coat.

3. Grill the meat, turning once and brushing with the remaining glaze, for 4 to 6 minutes until golden brown, slightly charred, and cooked to medium-rare (page 11). Transfer the skewers to a cutting board and let rest for 5 minutes.

4. Place the skewers on a platter and serve hot or at room temperature.

Green Chile Burgers

BOBBY
FLAY'S
GRILLING
FOR
LIFE

156

I was served a version of these cheeseburgers on a recent visit to New Mexico at a restaurant called La Casa Sena. Epazote and Chihuahua cheese are Mexican ingredients that add an authentic touch to this burger. Not to worry if you can't find them: Fresh oregano or cilantro can be used in place of epazote, and provolone cheese is a great substitute for the Chihuahua.

Serves 4

GREEN CHILE SAUCE
2 poblano chiles, grilled (page 25),
    peeled, seeded, and chopped
1 medium red onion, grilled (page 25)
    and chopped
2 cloves garlic, chopped
2 tablespoons chopped fresh epazote,
    oregano, or cilantro leaves
¼ cup cold water
¼ teaspoon kosher salt
¼ teaspoon freshly ground black pepper

Nutritional Analysis (per serving)

Calories: **500**	Protein (gm): **64**	Carbohydrates (gm): **30**
Total Sugar (gm): **7**	Total Fat (gm): **14**	Saturated Fat (gm): **7**
Cholesterol (mg): **120**	Sodium (mg): **621**	Fiber (gm): **3**

Combine all of the ingredients in a blender and blend until smooth. *The sauce can be made up to 8 hours in advance, covered, and kept refrigerated. Bring to room temperature before using.*

BURGERS

2 pounds ground beef, 90% to 95% lean

1 teaspoon kosher salt

1 teaspoon freshly ground black pepper

4 slices Chihuahua or provolone cheese, 1 ounce each

4 whole grain hamburger buns

4 romaine lettuce leaves

4 thick slices beefsteak tomato

4 Pickled Jalapeños (page 58), thinly sliced

1. Heat your grill to high.

2. Shape the ground beef with your hands into 4 round patties about 1½ inches thick and season each burger on both sides with the salt and pepper. Grill until charred on both sides and cooked to medium (page 11), about 8 minutes.

3. Place a slice of the cheese on each burger, close the lid or loosely cover with foil, and cook until the cheese has just melted, about 1 minute. Transfer to a cutting board and let rest for 5 minutes.

4. Place the burgers on the buns and top each with green chile sauce, lettuce, tomato, and pickled jalapeño before serving.

Black Pepper–Crusted Filet Mignon with Goat Cheese and Roasted Red Pepper–Ancho Salsa

While it is incredibly tender, filet mignon is not the most flavorful cut of beef. This crust and its accompaniments take care of that! If you are unfamiliar with ancho chiles, they are dried poblanos with a spicy raisin flavor. You can find them in many supermarkets and specialty markets, as well as online.

Serves 4

ROASTED RED PEPPER–ANCHO SALSA

2 ancho chiles

3 cloves garlic, coarsely chopped

2 tablespoons pine nuts

2 teaspoons honey

2 red bell peppers, grilled (page 25), peeled, seeded, and cut into ¼-inch-thick strips

3 tablespoons red wine vinegar

3 tablespoons chopped fresh cilantro leaves

¼ teaspoon kosher salt

¼ teaspoon freshly ground black pepper

Nutritional Analysis (per serving)

Calories: **540**	Protein (gm): **34**	Carbohydrates (gm): **8**
Total Sugar (gm): **2**	Total Fat (gm): **42**	Saturated Fat (gm): **15**
Cholesterol (mg): **107**	Sodium (mg): **407**	Fiber (gm): **2.6**

1. Place the ancho chiles in a medium bowl, cover with boiling water, and let sit at room temperature for 30 minutes.

2. Remove the chiles from the soaking liquid. Stem the chiles, coarsely chop, and combine in a blender with the garlic, pine nuts, honey, and ¼ cup of the soaking liquid. Blend until smooth.

3. Pour the mixture into a medium bowl and stir in the bell pepper strips, vinegar, cilantro, salt, and pepper. Cover and let sit at room temperature for at least 30 minutes and up to 4 hours before serving.

**BLACK PEPPER–CRUSTED FILET MIGNON
WITH GOAT CHEESE**

4 filets mignons, 5 ounces each
1 tablespoon canola oil
1 teaspoon kosher salt
4 teaspoons coarsely ground black pepper
4 ounces fresh goat cheese, cut into 4 slices
Cilantro leaves

1. Heat your grill to high.

2. Brush the filets with the oil and season both sides of each filet with the salt and one side of each filet with the black pepper. Place the steaks pepper side down on the grill and grill until lightly charred and crusty, 2 to 3 minutes. Turn the steaks over and grill for 2 to 3 minutes longer for medium-rare (page 11).

3. Top each filet with a slice of the cheese. Close the cover and grill until the cheese begins to melt slightly, about 1 minute.

4. Remove the steaks from the grill and let rest for 5 minutes. Top the filets with the salsa and garnish with cilantro leaves before serving.

Grilled Beef Filet
with Arugula and Parmesan

My favorite dishes are usually the simplest: Grill the filet, toss the arugula in olive oil and lemon juice, serve, and eat. That's it! Arugula is a great leafy green to use here but feel free to substitute another, such as spinach. Both have lots of cancer-fighting nutrients and are great sources of vitamin C.

Serves 6

6 filets mignons, 5 ounces each

4 tablespoons olive oil

1¼ teaspoons kosher salt

**1 teaspoon coarsely ground black pepper,
plus ¼ teaspoon freshly ground
black pepper**

Juice of 1 lemon

8 ounces arugula

½ medium red onion, thinly sliced

**4 ounces Parmigiano Reggiano cheese,
thinly shaved with a vegetable peeler**

Nutritional Analysis (per serving)

Calories: **515**   Protein (gm): **36**   Carbohydrates (gm): **4**

Total Sugar (gm): **1.5**   Total Fat (gm): **39**   Saturated Fat (gm): **14.5**

Cholesterol (mg): **105**   Sodium (mg): **613**   Fiber (gm): **1.4**

1. Heat your grill to high.

2. Brush each filet on both sides using 1 tablespoon of the oil and season with 1 teaspoon of the salt and all of the coarsely ground pepper. Grill until lightly charred and crusty, 2 to 3 minutes. Turn the steaks over and grill 2 to 3 minutes longer for medium-rare (page 11). Transfer the steaks to a cutting board and let rest for 5 minutes.

3. Meanwhile, whisk together the lemon juice and the remaining ¼ teaspoon salt and ¼ teaspoon pepper in a large bowl. Whisk in the remaining 3 tablespoons olive oil until emulsified. Add the arugula and onion and toss to coat.

4. Cut the meat into ¼-inch-thick slices and fan the meat around the rim of each of 6 plates. Mound the arugula salad in the center of the plates and garnish with the shaved Parmesan before serving.

Grilled T-Bone Steaks
with Garlic-Chile Oil

**BOBBY
FLAY'S
GRILLING
FOR
LIFE**

162

This is a simple way to bring lots of savory flavor to your table. Each ingredient—olive oil, garlic, fresh thyme, and red chile flakes—is distinctive and explosive. This steak is all about texture, hot and crusty outside and tender and juicy inside. The key? Don't play with your food as it cooks! Let it sit and form a crust and only turn it once. And, no matter how good it may smell when you pull it off of the grill, be sure to let the steak rest for at least 5 minutes before you slice it. You definitely won't want to sacrifice any of those juices to the cutting board.

Serves 6

¼ **cup olive oil**

6 cloves garlic, finely chopped

2 teaspoons chopped fresh thyme leaves

¼ **teaspoon red pepper flakes**

2 T-bone steaks, 1 pound each

2 teaspoons kosher salt

2 teaspoons freshly ground black pepper

1. Whisk together the oil, garlic, thyme, and red pepper flakes in a small bowl; set aside.

2. Heat your grill to high.

Nutritional Analysis (per serving)

Calories: **395**   Protein (gm): **41**   Carbohydrates (gm): **1**

Total Sugar (gm): **0**   Total Fat (gm): **24**   Saturated Fat (gm): **6.6**

Cholesterol (mg): **89**   Sodium (mg): **491**   Fiber (gm): **0**

3. Season both sides of the steaks with the salt and pepper. Place the steaks on the grill and grill until golden brown and slightly charred, 4 to 5 minutes. Turn the steaks over, lower the heat to medium, close the lid, and continue cooking for 6 to 7 minutes for medium-rare (page 11).

4. Remove the steaks from the grill and transfer to a cutting board. Let rest for 5 minutes, then cut into ¼-inch-thick slices. Transfer to a platter and drizzle with the chile oil.

Red Wine–Rosemary–Marinated Flank Steak with Lemony White Beans

The marinade for this steak is heady and robust. Rosemary provides an incredible amount of flavor and a little goes a long way. Be sure to slice the steak against the grain. Tahini, a sesame paste that is used a lot in Middle Eastern food, adds a nutty flavor and creamy consistency to the beans.

Serves 6

MARINATED FLANK STEAK

1½ cups dry red wine

1 small onion, coarsely chopped

4 cloves garlic, coarsely chopped

2 tablespoons olive oil

2 tablespoons coarsely chopped fresh
  rosemary leaves

1 tablespoon chopped fresh thyme leaves

1 flank steak, 2 pounds, trimmed of fat
  and cut crosswise into 2 pieces

Combine the wine, onion, garlic, oil, rosemary, and thyme in a large, shallow baking dish and stir to combine. Add the steak and turn to coat. Cover and refrigerate for at least 4 hours and up to 24 hours.

Nutritional Analysis (per serving)

Calories: **676**	Protein (gm): **48**	Carbohydrates (gm): **50**
Total Sugar (gm): **3**	Total Fat (gm): **30**	Saturated Fat (gm): **7**
Cholesterol (mg): **61**	Sodium (mg): **792**	Fiber (gm): **10**

LEMONY WHITE BEANS

2 cups canned white beans, rinsed and drained

6 cloves garlic, coarsely chopped

⅓ cup fresh lemon juice

1 teaspoon ground cumin

1 teaspoon kosher salt

¼ teaspoon freshly ground black pepper

¼ cup tahini

¼ cup olive oil

¼ cup finely chopped fresh flat-leaf parsley leaves

3 tablespoons finely chopped fresh mint leaves

Combine the beans, garlic, lemon juice, cumin, salt, and pepper in a food processor or blender and process until the beans are coarsely chopped. Add the tahini and oil and process until smooth. If the mixture appears dry and does not have a creamy consistency, add water a few tablespoons at a time until creamy. Scrape into a bowl and stir in the parsley and mint.

TO GRILL

1 teaspoon kosher salt

2 teaspoons freshly ground black pepper

6 whole wheat pita breads

1. Heat your grill to high.

2. Remove the meat from the marinade and season on both sides with the salt and pepper. Grill, turning once, for 12 to 14 minutes, until slightly charred and cooked to medium-rare (page 11). Transfer to a cutting board and let rest for 5 minutes.

3. Cut the meat against the grain into ½-inch-thick slices. Stuff the pitas with slices of the flank steak and a large dollop of the white beans.

Smoky and Fiery Skirt Steak with Avocado-Oregano Relish

BOBBY
FLAY'S
GRILLING
FOR
LIFE

166

Skirt steak is a chewy cut that's full of beefy flavor. It's the perfect vehicle for the big flavors of this dressing. The smokiness comes from the chipotle chiles, which are smoked jalapeños. Make them a staple in your pantry.

Serves 6

SMOKY AND FIERY DRESSING

¼ cup red wine vinegar

2 cloves garlic, chopped

2 chipotle chiles in adobo

1 teaspoon honey

¼ teaspoon kosher salt

¼ teaspoon freshly ground black pepper

½ cup canola oil

¼ cup finely chopped fresh cilantro leaves

Combine the vinegar, garlic, chiles, honey, salt, and pepper in a blender and blend until smooth. With the motor running, slowly drizzle in the oil and blend until emulsified. Add the cilantro and pulse 2 times just to incorporate.

Nutritional Analysis (per serving with 2 tablespoons relish)

Calories: **483**	Protein (gm): **31**	Carbohydrates (gm): **8.5**
Total Sugar (gm): **1.5**	Total Fat (gm): **36**	Saturated Fat (gm): **8.7**
Cholesterol (mg): **79**	Sodium (mg): **370**	Fiber (gm): **4**

AVOCADO-OREGANO RELISH

2 ripe Hass avocados, pitted, peeled,
  and coarsely chopped

½ medium red onion, finely chopped

Juice of 2 limes

2 tablespoons canola oil

1 tablespoon finely chopped fresh
  oregano leaves

¼ teaspoon kosher salt

¼ teaspoon freshly ground black pepper

Combine all of the ingredients in a medium bowl.

GRILLED SKIRT STEAK

2 pounds skirt steak, cut crosswise
  into 3 equal pieces

1 tablespoon canola oil

1 teaspoon kosher salt

2 teaspoons freshly ground black pepper

1. Heat your grill to high.

2. Brush the steak with the oil and season both sides with the salt and pepper. Grill, turning once, for 6 to 8 minutes until slightly charred and cooked to medium-rare (page 11). Transfer to a cutting board and let rest for 5 minutes.

3. Cut the meat against the grain into ½-inch-thick slices. Drizzle each serving with dressing and top with 2 tablespoons of the avocado relish. Serve the remaining relish on the side if desired.

Harissa-Marinated Lamb Skewers on Farro Salad with Pine Nuts and Goat Cheese

BOBBY
FLAY'S
GRILLING
FOR
LIFE

168

Although farro has been around for thousands of years, it recently became popular in this country as much for its taste as for its health benefits. This protein-rich grain has an incredibly rich, nutty flavor and a pleasant chewy texture that provides a perfect foil for the spicy marinade of the lamb skewers and the tangy flavor and creamy consistency of the goat cheese. Farro can be found in most supermarkets and health food stores. Harissa is a hot and spicy North African condiment made from chiles, garlic, cumin, coriander, and caraway seeds. Its wonderfully unique flavor works with lamb as well as beef, pork, and chicken. It can be found in specialty food stores in the spice section and online.

Serves 6

HARISSA-MARINATED LAMB

2 pounds lamb tenderloin

½ cup olive oil

2 tablespoons harissa

3 cloves garlic, finely chopped

1 tablespoon finely chopped fresh oregano leaves

Slice each lamb tenderloin lengthwise in half, then crosswise to make 24 equal pieces. Whisk together the oil, harissa, garlic, and oregano in a large bowl, add the lamb pieces, and toss to coat. Cover and refrigerate for at least 2 hours and up to 8 hours.

Nutritional Analysis (per serving)

Calories: **771**   Protein (gm): **45**   Carbohydrates (gm): **35**

Total Sugar (gm): **0**   Total Fat (gm): **49**   Saturated Fat (gm): **13**

Cholesterol (mg): **122**   Sodium (mg): **653**   Fiber (gm): **3**

FARRO SALAD

4½ cups water

1½ cups farro

1 tablespoon plus 1 teaspoon kosher salt

½ cup olive oil

3 tablespoons red wine vinegar

3 tablespoons finely chopped fresh mint leaves

6 ounces goat cheese, crumbled

2 tablespoons pine nuts, toasted (page 26)

½ teaspoon freshly ground black pepper

1. Combine the water, farro, and 1 tablespoon of the salt in a medium saucepan and bring to a boil over high heat. Reduce the heat to medium-low, cover the pot, and simmer until the farro is tender, 30 to 40 minutes.

2. Drain the farro well and transfer to a large bowl. Add the remaining ingredients and toss to combine. Keep warm or at room temperature.

TO GRILL

Twelve 6-inch wooden skewers, soaked in water for 30 minutes

1 teaspoon kosher salt

1 teaspoon freshly ground black pepper

1. Heat your grill to high.

2. Remove the lamb from the marinade and spear 2 pieces of lamb onto each skewer, keeping them together at one end of the skewer. (This will make the grilled skewer easier to hold and eat.) Season with the salt and pepper and grill the lamb, turning as needed, for 4 to 6 minutes for medium-rare (page 11). Remove to a cutting board and let rest for 5 minutes.

3. Transfer the farro salad to a large platter and arrange the skewers on top.

Grilled Lamb Chops and Oregano Vinaigrette with Radish Tzatziki

BOBBY
FLAY'S
GRILLING
FOR
LIFE

170

I have always loved Greek cuisine—it's all about simple, clean flavors. This Greek-inspired dish takes grilled lamb and dresses it up with flavorful condiments. Obviously, I have nothing against the classic cucumber tzatziki, but I love the subtle bite that radishes add to the tangy sauce. As for the vinaigrette, traditional Greek cuisine may call for dried oregano, but to my mind, you can't beat fresh. And fresh is what this dish and Greek food is all about.

Serves 4

RADISH TZATZIKI
¾ cup finely grated radishes
¼ small red onion, finely grated
¾ cup nonfat Greek yogurt
3 cloves garlic, finely chopped
2 teaspoons red wine vinegar
¼ teaspoon kosher salt
¼ teaspoon freshly ground black pepper

1. Place the radishes and onion in a medium strainer, place a small plate on top, and let sit over a bowl for 30 minutes to drain the excess liquid.

Nutritional Analysis (per serving with 2 tablespoons vinaigrette)

Calories: **613**   Protein (gm): **49**   Carbohydrates (gm): **8**

Total Sugar (gm): **6**   Total Fat (gm): **41**   Saturated Fat (gm): **10**

Cholesterol (mg): **150**   Sodium (mg): **605**   Fiber (gm): **0**

2. Transfer the drained radish mixture to a medium bowl, add the remaining ingredients, and mix well. Cover and refrigerate for at least 30 minutes and up to 1 day before serving.

OREGANO VINAIGRETTE

¼ cup red wine vinegar

3 tablespoons chopped fresh oregano leaves

2 cloves garlic, chopped

1 teaspoon honey

¼ teaspoon kosher salt

¼ teaspoon freshly ground black pepper

⅓ cup olive oil

Combine the vinegar, oregano, garlic, honey, salt, and pepper in a blender and blend until smooth. With the motor running, slowly drizzle in the oil and blend until emulsified.

GRILLED LAMB CHOPS

8 lamb rib chops, 4 ounces each

2 tablespoons olive oil

1 teaspoon kosher salt

1 teaspoon freshly ground black pepper

1. Heat your grill to high.

2. Brush the lamb chops on both sides with the oil and season with the salt and pepper. Grill the chops until lightly charred and crusty, 2 to 3 minutes. Turn the chops over and grill until cooked to medium-rare (page 11), 2 to 3 minutes longer.

3. Remove the chops to a platter and immediately drizzle each chop with 1 tablespoon of the oregano vinaigrette. Let rest for 5 minutes before serving.

4. Serve 2 chops per person with some radish tzatziki on the side. Serve the remaining vinaigrette on the side if desired.

Lamb Burgers with Tomato-Mint Salsa and Feta Cheese

**BOBBY
FLAY'S
GRILLING
FOR
LIFE**

172

This recipe takes three classic Greek ingredients—lamb, mint, and feta cheese—and turns them into a fantastic burger. Try slathering them with tangy yogurt instead of traditional ketchup and mustard, and set them atop whole wheat pitas instead of sesame-seed hamburger buns. You'll also find that these burgers make great hors d'oeuvres in miniature without any bread at all.

Serves 4

TOMATO-MINT SALSA

**2 ripe beefsteak tomatoes,
    finely chopped**

1 small red onion, finely chopped

1 jalapeño chile, finely chopped

Juice of 1 lime

1 teaspoon honey

**2 tablespoons finely chopped fresh
    mint leaves**

¼ teaspoon kosher salt

¼ teaspoon freshly ground black pepper

Nutritional Analysis (per serving)

Calories: **553**   Protein (gm): **58**   Carbohydrates (gm): **12**

Total Sugar (gm): **7.6**   Total Fat (gm): **29**   Saturated Fat (gm): **12**

Cholesterol (mg): **205**   Sodium (mg): **999**   Fiber (gm): **3**

Combine all of the ingredients in a bowl and let sit at room temperature for at least 30 minutes and up to 1 hour before serving. *The salsa can be made 1 day in advance, covered, and kept refrigerated. Bring to room temperature before serving.*

LAMB BURGERS

1½ pounds ground lamb, 90% to 95% lean

1 tablespoon ground cumin

½ teaspoon kosher salt

1 teaspoon freshly ground black pepper

2 tablespoons canola oil

8 ounces feta cheese, crumbled

1. Heat your grill to high.

2. Mix together the lamb, cumin, salt, and pepper in a bowl. Shape the mixture with your hands into 4 round patties about 1½ inches thick. Brush the burgers on both sides with the oil. Grill the burgers for 2 to 3 minutes per side until slightly charred and cooked to medium (page 11). Divide the cheese among the burgers, close the lid of the grill, and cook an additional minute to slightly melt the cheese.

3. Top each burger with a large spoonful of the tomato-mint salsa before serving.

Souvlaki with Merguez Sausage and Piquillo Pepper–Yogurt Sauce

This is an old-fashioned Greek dish with a distinctly Spanish twist. I thought that a trip to the other side of the Mediterranean could only improve this souvlaki, so I added Spanish roasted peppers and Merguez sausage (spicy lamb sausage available in specialty markets and online at www.dartagnan.com). The smokiness of the piquillo peppers goes extremely well with the tangy yogurt. Whole wheat pitas may not be traditional, but they are a solid, healthy choice.

Serves 8

SOUVLAKI

¼ cup olive oil

6 cloves garlic, chopped

1 medium yellow onion, coarsely chopped

1 tablespoon chopped fresh oregano leaves

2 pounds lamb tenderloin, cut into
    1-inch cubes

Stir together the oil, garlic, onion, and oregano in a large bowl, add the lamb, and toss to coat. Cover and marinate in the refrigerator for at least 1 hour and up to 8 hours.

Nutritional Analysis (per serving)

Calories: **687**   Protein (gm): **57**   Carbohydrates (gm): **55**

Total Sugar (gm): **5**   Total Fat (gm): **27**   Saturated Fat (gm): **9**

Cholesterol (mg): **155**   Sodium (mg): **699**   Fiber (gm): **7**

PIQUILLO PEPPER-YOGURT SAUCE

1¼ cups nonfat Greek yogurt

4 piquillo peppers, drained, or 1 red bell pepper,
    grilled (page 25), peeled, seeded, and chopped

6 cloves garlic

2 teaspoons grated lemon zest

1 tablespoon chopped fresh oregano leaves

¼ teaspoon kosher salt

¼ teaspoon freshly ground black pepper

Combine all of the ingredients in a blender and blend until smooth. Transfer to a small bowl, cover, and refrigerate for at least 30 minutes and up to 4 hours before serving.

TO GRILL

2 red bell peppers

1 yellow onion, sliced ¼ inch thick

2 tablespoons olive oil

1½ teaspoons kosher salt

1½ teaspoons freshly ground black pepper

12 ounces Merguez or hot Italian sausages

Sixteen 6-inch wooden skewers, soaked
    in water for at least 30 minutes

8 whole wheat pita breads

1. Heat your grill to high.

2. Brush the peppers and onion with the oil and season with ½ teaspoon of the salt and ½ teaspoon of the pepper. Grill the peppers until charred on all sides, 8 to 10 minutes. Place the grilled peppers in a bowl, cover with plastic wrap, and let sit for 15 minutes. Grill the onion until golden brown and slightly charred on each side, 3 to 4 minutes per side. Remove to a plate and keep warm.

3. Grill the sausages until golden brown on all sides, about 6 minutes. Transfer the sausages to a cutting board and let rest for 5 minutes before cutting into 1-inch pieces. (The sausage may still be pink in the center but will cook through when you return it to the grill with the lamb.)

4. Remove the lamb from the marinade. Skewer the lamb and sausage onto the skewers and season with the remaining 1 teaspoon salt and 1 teaspoon pepper. Grill, turning as needed, until the lamb is slightly charred and cooked to medium-rare (page 11), about 4 minutes. Transfer to a cutting board and let rest for 5 minutes.

5. Peel, halve, and seed the peppers. Cut into strips.

6. Grill the pita on both sides for about 20 seconds just to warm through. Cut off 1-inch from the top of each pita. Remove the lamb and sausage from the skewers and stuff the meat into the pitas. Add some of the onion and peppers, then drizzle with the yogurt sauce before serving.

Yogurt-Mint-Marinated Grilled Leg of Lamb

**BOBBY
FLAY'S
GRILLING
FOR
LIFE**

178

Here the yogurt provides the lamb with more than just its incredible flavor and health benefits (protein and calcium to name a few); it also tenderizes the meat and helps to form a fantastic crust on the grill! This recipe would be perfect paired with Grilled Asparagus and Egg Salad with Tarragon-Caper Vinaigrette (page 30) for a spring dinner.

Serves 8

1 boneless leg of lamb, about 5 pounds,
    trimmed of excess fat

5 cloves garlic, thinly sliced

2 cups nonfat Greek yogurt

½ cup fresh mint leaves

2 teaspoons ground cumin

3 to 5 dashes Tabasco sauce

2 teaspoons kosher salt

2 teaspoons freshly ground black pepper

1. Using a paring knife, make small slits over the entire surface of the lamb and stuff with the sliced garlic. Place the lamb on a rimmed baking sheet.

Nutritional Analysis (per serving)

Calories: **397**   Protein (gm): **61**   Carbohydrates (gm): **5**

Total Sugar (gm): **3.7**   Total Fat (gm): **13**   Saturated Fat (gm): **4.6**

Cholesterol (mg): **182**   Sodium (mg): **325**   Fiber (gm): **0**

2. Combine the yogurt, mint, cumin, and Tabasco sauce in the bowl of a food processor or in a blender and process until smooth. Pour the marinade over the lamb and rub the mixture into the meat. Cover and refrigerate for at least 8 hours and up to overnight.

3. Heat your grill to high.

4. Season the lamb with the salt and pepper. Place the lamb boned side up on the grill and grill until golden brown and slightly charred, 4 to 5 minutes. Turn the lamb over, reduce the heat of the grill to medium (aim to maintain a constant temperature of 350 degrees F), and grill until a thermometer inserted into the meat reaches a temperature of 135 degrees F for medium-rare, 1¼ to 1½ hours more. (*If using a charcoal grill:* After 45 minutes, add about 2 dozen hot coals to maintain the heat.)

5. Transfer to a cutting board and let rest for 10 minutes. Cut the meat on a diagonal into ¼-inch-thick slices. Serve hot, at room temperature, or chilled. *Leftovers will keep, tightly covered, in the refrigerator for up to 2 days.*

DRINKS AND DESSERTS

You may be thinking, "*Healthy desserts? Isn't that an oxymoron?*" When I first faced this chapter, I thought it was going to be tough because I knew that I wasn't about to start calling for soy flour or sugar substitutes. But neither turned out to be necessary. With nutritious whole fruits and crunchy, protein-filled nuts, I created excellent desserts that aren't loaded with refined sugar. Grilled Plums with Spiced Walnut-Yogurt Sauce, Pomegranate Margaritas, Strawberries with Ricotta Cream—delicious! These straightforward recipes require no baking, and yet all are incredibly tasty. Just a note: The sugar counts in some of these recipes may seem a bit high. Remember, though, that the majority of the sugar is coming from whole fruits, which have a high nutritional value.

Cantaloupe-Mint Agua Fresca (Mexican Fruit Cooler)

Totally refreshing, this cool drink isn't overly sweet. It tastes of pure cantaloupe and mint. It is really important that you use very ripe cantaloupe for this drink. If it's not available, honeydew melon or fresh berries are a perfect substitute. Should you want to spice things up, add a splash of vodka or tequila.

Serves 4

1 cup very cold water
1 cup crushed ice
3 cups chopped very ripe cantaloupe
2 tablespoons chopped fresh mint leaves
4 mint sprigs

Combine all of the ingredients except for the mint sprigs in a blender and blend until smooth. Pour into 4 glasses and garnish with the mint sprigs.

Nutritional Analysis (per serving)

Calories: **41**   Protein (gm): **1**   Carbohydrates (gm): **10**

Total Sugar (gm): **9**   Total Fat (gm): **0**   Saturated Fat (gm): **0**

Cholesterol (mg): **0**   Sodium (mg): **19**   Fiber (gm): **1**

Green Tea Mint Iced Tea

Refreshing, healthy, and delicious. If you need it sweetened, I recommend adding a little simple syrup or honey. In addition to its antioxidant properties, green tea is thought to boost metabolism.

Serves 4

5 cups cold water
6 green tea bags
¼ cup tightly packed fresh mint leaves
Ice

1. Bring the water to a boil in a medium saucepan, remove from the heat, and add the tea bags. Cover and let steep for 4 minutes. Remove the tea bags, stir in the mint, and let steep for 30 minutes.

2. Strain the mixture into a pitcher and serve over ice.

SIMPLE SYRUP

Combine equal parts sugar and water in a saucepan and bring to a boil. Simmer for 1 minute until the sugar is melted. Remove from the heat and let cool to room temperature. *The syrup will keep, covered in the refrigerator, for 30 days.*

Nutritional Analysis (per serving without sugar)

Calories: **3.5**   Protein (gm): **0**   Carbohydrates (gm): **1**

Total Sugar (gm): **0**   Total Fat (gm): **0**   Saturated Fat (gm): **0**

Cholesterol (mg): **0**   Sodium (mg): **0**   Fiber (gm): **0**

Pomegranate Margarita

BOBBY
FLAY'S
GRILLING
FOR
LIFE

184

Pomegranates have become popular recently, and pomegranate juice has hit the shelves with a bang over the past year. Not only are pomegranates chock-full of antioxidants, but they also make a totally refreshing margarita—tart and sweet!

Serves 1

2 tablespoons fresh lime juice
2 tablespoons plus 1 teaspoon fresh
   pomegranate seeds
¼ cup silver tequila
Crushed ice
Lime slice

Combine the lime juice and 2 tablespoons of the pomegranate seeds in a rocks glass. Using the bottom of a wooden spoon, mash the pomegranate seeds into the juice. Stir in the tequila and add crushed ice. Top with a slice of lime and the remaining 1 teaspoon pomegranate seeds.

Nutritional Analysis (per serving)

Calories: **155**   Protein (gm): **0**   Carbohydrates (gm): **7.5**

Total Sugar (gm): **4**   Total Fat (gm): **0**   Saturated Fat (gm): **0**

Cholesterol (mg): **0**   Sodium (mg): **0**   Fiber (gm): **0**

White Nectarine Bellini

There's no need to fly to Venice just to get your Bellini fix at Harry's Bar. Make them at home! Although these are classically made with fresh peaches, I like to substitute ripe white nectarines when in season. Purée the nectarines, top with prosecco, and you are good to go. Try these instead of mimosas at your next brunch.

Serves 4

2 very ripe white nectarines
4 cups prosecco or other sparkling wine,
    chilled

1. Halve and pit the nectarines. Cut 4 thin slices from one of the halves and set aside to use as a garnish. Coarsely chop the remaining nectarines, combine with a few tablespoons of water in a blender, and blend until smooth.

2. Divide the purée among 4 chilled champagne flutes, fill to the top with prosecco, and stir gently to combine. Garnish each glass with a nectarine wedge.

Nutritional Analysis (per serving)

Calories: **198**   Protein (gm): **1**   Carbohydrates (gm): **13**

Total Sugar (gm): **5**   Total Fat (gm): **0**   Saturated Fat (gm): **0**

Cholesterol (mg): **0**   Sodium (mg): **0**   Fiber (gm): **1**

Grilled Apricots
with Bittersweet Chocolate and Almonds

BOBBY
FLAY'S
GRILLING
FOR
LIFE

186

Most people only think of apricots in their dried form, but fresh apricots are a real summertime treat. If you can't find them, nectarines and peaches are another good way to go.

Serves 4

8 ripe fresh apricots, halved and pitted
1 tablespoon canola oil
2 ounces bittersweet chocolate, melted
¼ cup sliced almonds, toasted (page 26)

1. Heat your grill to high.

2. Brush the apricots on both sides with the oil and grill cut side down for 2 to 3 minutes until slightly charred. Turn them over and grill for 1 to 2 minutes until just heated through.

3. Divide the apricot halves among 4 bowls. Drizzle each serving with melted chocolate and sprinkle with almonds.

Nutritional Analysis (per serving)

Calories: **244**   Protein (gm): **6**   Carbohydrates (gm): **19**

Total Sugar (gm): **13**   Total Fat (gm): **18.5**   Saturated Fat (gm): **4**

Cholesterol (mg): **0**   Sodium (mg): **0**   Fiber (gm): **4.5**

Strawberries with Ricotta Cream

This is a classic way to highlight one of summer's greatest pleasures—a bowl of perfectly ripe strawberries. Strawberries Romanoff is normally made with sour cream, but I like the slightly sweet taste of ricotta better. This dessert is simple, but the result is truly elegant.

Serves 4

1 cup part-skim ricotta cheese or low-fat sour cream
1 tablespoon light brown sugar
2 tablespoons orange liqueur, such as Grand Marnier,
    or fresh orange juice
1 pint strawberries, hulled and sliced

1. Place the ricotta in a small strainer set over a bowl and refrigerate for 30 minutes to drain the excess liquid.

2. Transfer the drained ricotta to a food processor or blender, add the brown sugar and orange liqueur, and process until smooth. *The ricotta mixture can be made up to 8 hours in advance, covered, and kept refrigerated.*

3. Divide the strawberries among 4 dessert bowls and top each serving with a ¼ cup of the ricotta mixture.

Nutritional Analysis (per serving)
Calories: **140**   Protein (gm): **7**   Carbohydrates (gm): **13**
Total Sugar (gm): **8**   Total Fat (gm): **5**   Saturated Fat (gm): **3**
Cholesterol (mg): **19**   Sodium (mg): **78**   Fiber (gm): **1.5**

Grilled Plums
with Spiced Walnut-Yogurt Sauce

Fresh orange juice and orange zest sweeten yogurt just enough to make a dessert sauce for grilled summer sweet plums. Cinnamon and nutmeg add a subtle spice, while toasted walnuts create texture and additional richness for the perfect topping.

Serves 4

SPICED WALNUT-YOGURT SAUCE
1 cup nonfat Greek yogurt
2 tablespoons fresh orange juice
1 teaspoon grated orange zest
¼ teaspoon ground cinnamon
⅛ teaspoon freshly grated nutmeg
¼ cup walnuts, toasted (page 26),
   coarsely chopped

Whisk together the yogurt, orange juice, zest, cinnamon, and nutmeg in a small bowl. Cover and refrigerate for at least 30 minutes and up to 8 hours before serving. Just before serving, stir in the walnuts.

Nutritional Analysis (per serving)

Calories: **152**   Protein (gm): **6**   Carbohydrates (gm): **18**

Total Sugar (gm): **15**   Total Fat (gm): **7**   Saturated Fat (gm): **0**

Cholesterol (mg): **0**   Sodium (mg): **47**   Fiber (gm): **2**

6 plums, halved and pitted

2 teaspoons canola oil

1. Heat your grill to high.

2. Brush the cut sides of the plums with the oil. Place the plums cut side down on the grill and grill for 2 to 3 minutes until golden brown and slightly caramelized. Turn over and grill until just heated through, 1 minute longer.

3. Place 3 plum halves in each bowl and top with the yogurt sauce.

Grilled Figs
with Vanilla-Orange Crème Fraîche and Toasted Pistachios

Grilling fruit has become more and more popular and with good reason. The heat of the grill brings out the natural sugars in fruit and creates a caramelized crust, making grilled fresh figs one of a kind. Their honeylike sweetness is complemented by tangy crème fraîche.

Serves 4

VANILLA-ORANGE CRÈME FRAÎCHE
½ cup crème fraîche
2 tablespoons fresh orange juice
1 teaspoon finely grated orange zest
1 teaspoon pure vanilla extract

Whisk together all the ingredients. Cover and refrigerate for at least 1 hour and up to 1 day before serving.

Nutritional Analysis (per serving)

Calories: **298**   Protein (gm): **4**   Carbohydrates (gm): **32**

Total Sugar (gm): **25**   Total Fat (gm): **18**   Saturated Fat (gm): **8**

Cholesterol (mg): **25**   Sodium (mg): **81**   Fiber (gm): **5**

GRILLED FIGS

12 black Mission figs
1 tablespoon canola oil
¼ cup chopped pistachios, toasted (page 26)

1. Heat your grill to medium.

2. Brush the figs with the oil and grill until golden brown on both sides, 4 to 5 minutes total.

3. Divide the figs among 4 dessert bowls, top with a dollop of the crème fraîche, and sprinkle with pistachios.

Mix and Match

The great thing about the vinaigrettes, relishes, and sauces in this book is their versatility. Recipes are just guides. You can switch around the proteins and still have wonderful flavor combinations. Of course, not all vinaigrettes, relishes, and sauces can be used on all fish and meats. Some of them are too light and will get lost on the strong flavor of beef or lamb, and some of them are too strong and will totally overwhelm the mild taste of fish or poultry. The options listed below aren't too strong or too mild. They're just right.

FISH

Sage-Orange Vinaigrette (page 122)

Sage-Lemon Pesto (page 134)

Red Pepper–Tahini Vinaigrette (page 81)

Mustard-Dill Vinaigrette (page 70)

Caper-Basil Vinaigrette (page 54)

Grilled Pepper and Black Olive Relish (page 100)

CHICKEN AND TURKEY

Green Onion Vinaigrette (page 50)

Green Romesco Sauce (page 98)

Fennel-Tomatillo Relish (page 112)

Garlic–Red Chile–Thyme Marinade (page 66)

Tarragon-Caper Vinaigrette (page 30)

Lemon-Garlic Aïoli (page 56)

Grapefruit-Thyme Mojo (page 96)

Mango Pico de Gallo (page 78)

BEEF AND LAMB

Anchovy Vinaigrette (page 101)

Gorgonzola Vinaigrette (page 32)

Green Romesco Sauce (page 98)

Black Pepper–Sweet Mustard Sauce (page 140)

Green Chile–Cilantro Sauce (page 124)

Jalapeño Pesto (page 84)

Mustard–Green Onion Sauce (page 128)

MIX AND
MATCH

194

Meals in Minutes

As you read this book, you soon will realize that the majority of my recipes are easy to prepare. I do that for two reasons: One is that the majority of grilling is done during the warm months when the last thing you want to do is stand in front of a hot grill or stove for hours. The second reason is that today everyone, like myself, is busy working long hours and raising families. No one has the time to prepare meals with long lists of ingredients and pages of instruction. I want to create really flavorful, nutritious food that can be made in a short amount of time. Of course, there are a few recipes that do require more ingredients and preparation than others, and those can be put together on weekends and for special occasions when you want to pull out all the stops. But when time *isn't* on your side and you need a healthy lunch or dinner in minutes, try the ideas below:

MENU I

Grilled Chicken Cutlets with Lemon and Black Pepper and Arugula-Tomato
    Salad (page 120)

Strawberries with Ricotta Cream (page 187)

MENU II

Grilled and Marinated Zucchini and Yellow Squash (page 34)

Garlic–Red Chile–Thyme–Marinated Shrimp (page 66)

MENU III

Grilled Tuna Salad Sandwiches with Lemon-Habanero Mayonnaise (page 110)

Cantaloupe-Mint Agua Fresca (page 182)

MENU IV

Grilled Asian-Style Eggplant Salad (page 36)

Pork Tenderloin Crusted with Green Onion, Jalapeño, and Ginger (page 144)

Green Tea Mint Iced Tea (page 183)

MENU V

Grilled Spice-Rubbed Vidalia Onions (page 52)

Grilled Beef Filet with Arugula and Parmesan (page 160)

Grilled Apricots with Bittersweet Chocolate and Almonds (page 186)

MEALS IN
MINUTES

196

Party Foods

I love a good party, and just because I'm the one usually cooking doesn't mean that I am going to miss out on any of the fun. That's the great thing about the grill—it always seems to become the focal point of any good get-together. People gather around, drinks in hand, and check out the action.

There's nothing fussy about a party built around the grill—just good times with friends enjoying great food. Don't worry about individual plates or courses. I think that good friends are just as important as family, and the best way to serve family is family style. Put together some beautiful platters of grilled food and watch them pounce.

I also include lots of recipes in these menus that are best served at room temperature, so you can get the majority of the work done before your guests arrive. Hey, they didn't just come for the food, you know. They came to see you. So get out of the kitchen and behind the grill. I smell a party on the horizon!

BURGER PARTY

Green Chile Burgers (page 156)

Grilled Tuna Burgers with Green Onion Mayonnaise and Watercress (page 114)

Grilled Turkey Burgers with Monterey Jack, Poblano Pickle Relish, and Avocado
  Mayonnaise (page 132)

Pickled Jalapeños (page 58)

Grilled Spice-Rubbed Vidalia Onions (page 52)

Red Cabbage and Beet Slaw (page 48)

COCKTAIL PARTY

Grilled Oysters with Mango Pico de Gallo and Red Chile Horseradish (page 78)

Grilled Clams on the Half-Shell with Bacon, Garlic, and Hot Pepper (page 76)

Grilled Shrimp in Lettuce Leaves with Serrano-Mint Sauce (page 74)

Garlic-Mustard-Grilled Beef Skewers (page 154)

Pomegranate Margaritas (page 184)

ITALIAN FEAST

Twice-Grilled Peppers with Buffalo Mozzarella and Caper-Basil Vinaigrette
(page 54)

Grilled and Marinated Zucchini and Yellow Squash (page 34)

Grilled Halibut with Grilled Eggplant Salad (page 90)

Grilled Chicken Breasts with Fontina and Prosciutto with Sage-Orange
Vinaigrette (page 122)

White Nectarine Bellini (page 185)

MEDITERRANEAN NIGHTS

Grilled Fennel and Orange Salad with Almonds and Mint (page 40)

Grilled New Potatoes with Lemon-Garlic Aïoli and Chives (page 56)

Spanish-Spiced Chicken with Mustard–Green Onion Sauce (page 128)

Grilled Lamb Chops and Oregano Vinaigrette with Radish Tzatziki
(page 170)

Grilled Figs with Vanilla-Orange Crème Fraîche and Toasted Pistachios
(page 190)

NEW AMERICAN

Grilled Zucchini Succotash (page 38)

Grilled Spice-Rubbed Vidalia Onions (page 52)

Grilled Brook Trout with Horseradish and Tarragon Tartar Sauce (page 106)

Smoky and Fiery Skirt Steak with Avocado-Oregano Relish (page 166)

Strawberries with Ricotta Cream (page 187)

Sources

BARBECUE WOOD, CHIPS, AND PLANKS

www.barbecuewood.com, 509-961-3420

www.justsmokedsalmon.com, 866-716-2710

DRIED CHILES AND HOT SAUCES

www.kitchenmarket.com, 212-243-4433

SPICES

www.kalustyan.com, 908-688-6111

www.penzeys.com

CHEESES

www.dairysection.com

FRESH LOBSTERS

www.mainelobsterdirect.com, 800-556-2783

www.thelobsternet.com, 800-360-9520

FRESH SEAFOOD

www.gortonsfreshseafood.com

ORGANIC CHICKEN

www.eberlypoultry.com, 717-336-6440

DUCK AND GAME

www.dartagnan.com, 800-327-8426

MIDDLE EASTERN AND INDIAN INGREDIENTS

www.ethnicgrocer.com, 866-438-4642

WHOLE-GRAIN PRODUCTS

www.bobsredmill.com, 800-349-2173

SPECIALTY PRODUCE, SUCH AS BANANA LEAVES AND CHILES

www.melissas.com, 800-588-0151

SPANISH INGREDIENTS, SUCH AS PIQUILLO PEPPERS

www.tienda.com, 888-472-1022

SOURCES

200

KITCHEN SUPPLIES

www.broadwaypanhandler.com

www.williams-sonoma.com

GRILLING ACCESSORIES

www.bbqgalore.com, 800-752-3085

Index

allspice, 15
Grilled Jerk-Rubbed Grouper
with Hot Vinegar Sauce,
94–95
almonds
Grilled Apricots with Bittersweet
Chocolate and Almonds, 186
Grilled Fennel and Orange
Salad with Almonds and Mint,
40–41
Grilled Red Snapper with Green
Romesco Sauce, 98–99
anchovies
Grilled Salmon with Anchovy
Vinaigrette and Grilled Pep-
per and Black Olive Relish,
100–101
Tuna au Poivre Salad with
Creamy Tarragon-Garlic
Vinaigrette, 116–17
Antipasto, Grilled, with Gorgonzola
Vinaigrette, 32–33
Apricots, Grilled, with Bittersweet
Chocolate and Almonds, 186
arugula
Grilled Beef Filet with Arugula
and Parmesan, 160–61
Grilled Chicken Cutlets with
Lemon and Black Pepper and
Arugula-Tomato Salad,
120–21
asparagus
Grilled Antipasto with Gor-
gonzola Vinaigrette, 32–33
Grilled Asparagus and Egg
Salad with Tarragon-Caper
Vinaigrette, 30–31
avocados
Grilled Sea Scallops with
Avocado Vinaigrette and
Jalapeño Pesto, 84–85
Grilled Turkey Burgers with
Monterey Jack, Poblano Pickle
Relish, and Avocado
Mayonnaise, 132–33
Smoky and Fiery Skirt Steak
with Avocado-Oregano Relish,
166–67

bacon
Grilled Clams on the Half-Shell
with Bacon, Garlic, and Hot
Pepper, 76–77
Grilled German Sweet Potato
Salad, 42–43
Balsamic-Thyme-Glazed Duck
Breasts, 138–39
banana leaves, Yucatán Marinated
Halibut in Banana Leaves with
Pineapple-Orange Relish,
92–93
"Barbecued" Mahimahi with
Yellow Pepper–Cilantro Pesto,
88–89
bar towels, 10
basil, 13
Grilled and Marinated Zucchini
and Yellow Squash, 34–35
Grilled Asian-Style Eggplant
Salad, 36–37
Twice-Grilled Peppers with
Buffalo Mozzarella and Caper-
Basil Vinaigrette, 54–55
Whole Sea Bass with Charred
Serrano–Basil Vinaigrette,
104–5
beef
Black Pepper–Crusted Filet
Mignon with Goat Cheese and
Roasted Red Pepper–Ancho
Salsa, 158–59
Garlic-Mustard-Grilled Beef
Skewers, 154–55
Green Chile Burgers, 156–57
Grilled Beef Filet with Arugula
and Parmesan, 160–61
Grilled T-Bone Steaks with
Garlic-Chile Oil, 162–63
Red Wine–Rosemary–Marinated
Flank Steak with Lemony
White Beans, 164–65
Smoky and Fiery Skirt Steak with
Avocado-Oregano Relish,
166–67
beets, Red Cabbage and Beet Slaw,
48–49
Bellini, White Nectarine, 185

bell peppers
"Barbecued" Mahimahi with
Yellow Pepper–Cilantro Pesto,
88–89
Black Pepper–Crusted Filet
Mignon with Goat Cheese and
Roasted Red Pepper–Ancho
Salsa, 158–59
Cumin Grilled Sea Scallops with
Chickpea Salad and Red
Pepper–Tahini Vinaigrette,
80–82
Grilled Antipasto with Gor-
gonzola Vinaigrette, 32–33
Grilled Chicken Breasts Stuffed
with Goat Cheese with Green
Chile–Cilantro Sauce, 124–25
Grilled Prawns with Spicy Fresh
Pepper Sauce, 68–69
Grilled Red Snapper with Green
Romesco Sauce, 98–99
Grilled Salmon with Anchovy
Vinaigrette and Grilled
Pepper and Black Olive
Relish, 100–101
roasting, 25
Souvlaki with Merguez Sausage
and Piquillo Pepper–Yogurt
Sauce, 174–76
Twice-Grilled Peppers with
Buffalo Mozzarella and Caper-
Basil Vinaigrette, 54–55
Black Pepper–Crusted Filet
Mignon with Goat Cheese and
Roasted Red Pepper–Ancho
Salsa, 158–59
blanching vegetables, 26–27
Bricked Rosemary Chicken with
Lemon, 136–37
brushes
glaze and sauce, 8
grill, 8
Buckwheat Pizza with Cilantro
Pesto, Jack Cheese, and
Grilled Shrimp, 62–64
Bulgur Salad with Green Onion
Vinaigrette, 50–51
burgers. See sandwiches

cabbage
  Chinese Chicken Salad with Red
    Chile–Peanut Dressing, 126–27
  Pork Satay with Red Chile–
    Peanut Sauce and Napa
    Cabbage–Green Onion Slaw,
    148–50
  Red Cabbage and Beet Slaw,
    48–49
Cantaloupe-Mint Agua Fresca
  (Mexican Fruit Cooler), 182
capers, 24
  Grilled Asparagus and Egg
    Salad with Tarragon-Caper
    Vinaigrette, 30–31
  Grilled Halibut with Grilled
    Eggplant Salad, 90–91
  Grilled Salmon with Lemon,
    Dill, and Caper Vinaigrette,
    102–3
  Twice-Grilled Peppers with
    Buffalo Mozzarella and Caper-
    Basil Vinaigrette, 54–55
charcoal grills, 6, 7
cheese
  "Barbecued" Mahimahi with
    Yellow Pepper–Cilantro Pesto,
    88–89
  Black Pepper–Crusted Filet
    Mignon with Goat Cheese and
    Roasted Red Pepper–Ancho
    Salsa, 158–59
  Buckwheat Pizza with Cilantro
    Pesto, Jack Cheese, and
    Grilled Shrimp, 62–64
  Greek Orzo and Grilled Shrimp
    Salad with Mustard-Dill
    Vinaigrette, 70–71
  Green Chile Burgers, 156–57
  Grilled Antipasto with
    Gorgonzola Vinaigrette, 32–33
  Grilled Beef Filet with Arugula
    and Parmesan, 160–61
  Grilled Chicken Breasts with
    Fontina and Prosciutto with
    Sage-Orange Vinaigrette,
    122–23
  Grilled Chicken Breasts Stuffed
    with Goat Cheese with
    Green Chile–Cilantro Sauce,
    124–25
  Grilled Chicken Tenders with
    Spicy Chipotle Sauce and
    Blue Cheese–Yogurt Sauce,
    130–31

cheese (*cont.*)
  Grilled Portobello Mushrooms
    Stacked with Spinach and
    Manchego Cheese, 46–47
  Grilled Turkey Burgers with
    Monterey Jack, Poblano Pickle
    Relish, and Avocado
    Mayonnaise, 132–33
  Grilled Turkey Cutlets and
    Sage-Lemon Pesto, 134–35
  Grilled Zucchini Succotash,
    38–39
  Harissa-Marinated Lamb
    Skewers on Farro Salad with
    Pine Nuts and Goat Cheese,
    168–69
  Strawberries with Ricotta Cream,
    187
  Twice-Grilled Peppers with
    Buffalo Mozzarella and Caper-
    Basil Vinaigrette, 54–55
chicken
  Bricked Rosemary Chicken with
    Lemon, 136–37
  butterflying, 137
  Chinese Chicken Salad with
    Red Chile–Peanut Dressing,
    126–27
  Grilled Chicken Breasts with
    Fontina and Prosciutto with
    Sage-Orange Vinaigrette,
    122–23
  Grilled Chicken Breasts Stuffed
    with Goat Cheese with
    Green Chile–Cilantro Sauce,
    124–25
  Grilled Chicken Cutlets with
    Lemon and Black Pepper
    and Arugula-Tomato Salad,
    120–21
  Grilled Chicken Tenders with
    Spicy Chipotle Sauce and
    Blue Cheese–Yogurt Sauce,
    130–31
  Spanish-Spiced Chicken with
    Mustard–Green Onion Sauce,
    128–29
chickpeas, Cumin Grilled Sea
  Scallops with Chickpea Salad
  and Red Pepper–Tahini Vinai-
  grette, 80–82
chile powder
  "Barbecued" Mahimahi with
    Yellow Pepper–Cilantro Pesto,
    88–89

chile powder (*cont.*)
  Grilled Chicken Tenders with
    Spicy Chipotle Sauce and
    Blue Cheese–Yogurt Sauce,
    130–31
  Grilled Jerk-Rubbed Grouper
    with Hot Vinegar Sauce,
    94–95
  Grilled Spice-Rubbed Vidalia
    Onions, 52–53
  Grilled Tuna with Fennel-
    Tomatillo Relish, 112–13
  Pork Satay with Red Chile–
    Peanut Sauce and Napa
    Cabbage–Green Onion Slaw,
    148–50
  Yucatán Marinated Halibut in
    Banana Leaves with
    Pineapple-Orange Relish,
    92–93
chiles
  Black Pepper–Crusted Filet
    Mignon with Goat Cheese and
    Roasted Red Pepper–Ancho
    Salsa, 158–59
  Bulgur Salad with Green Onion
    Vinaigrette, 50–51
  Chinese Chicken Salad with Red
    Chile–Peanut Dressing,
    126–27
  Cumin Grilled Sea Scallops with
    Chickpea Salad and Red
    Pepper–Tahini Vinaigrette,
    80–82
  Garlic–Red Chile–Thyme–Mari-
    nated Shrimp, 66–67
  Green Chile Burgers, 156–57
  Grilled Chicken Breasts Stuffed
    with Goat Cheese with Green
    Chile–Cilantro Sauce, 124–25
  Grilled Chicken Tenders with
    Spicy Chipotle Sauce and
    Blue Cheese–Yogurt Sauce,
    130–31
  Grilled Jerk-Rubbed Grouper
    with Hot Vinegar Sauce,
    94–95
  Grilled Lobster Tails with Hot
    Ginger–Green Onion Vinai-
    grette, 86–87
  Grilled Oysters with Mango Pico
    de Gallo and Red Chile
    Horseradish, 78–79
  Grilled Prawns with Spicy Fresh
    Pepper Sauce, 68–69

chiles (*cont.*)

  Grilled Red Snapper with
    Grapefruit-Thyme Mojo, 96–97

  Grilled Red Snapper with Green
    Romesco Sauce, 98–99

  Grilled Sea Scallops with
    Avocado Vinaigrette and
    Jalapeño Pesto, 84–85

  Grilled Shrimp Escabeche,
    72–73

  Grilled Shrimp in Lettuce Leaves
    with Serrano–Mint Sauce,
    74–75

  Grilled Tuna Salad Sandwiches
    with Lemon-Habanero
    Mayonnaise, 110–11

  Grilled Tuna with Fennel-
    Tomatillo Relish, 112–13

  Grilled Turkey Burgers with
    Monterey Jack, Poblano Pickle
    Relish, and Avocado
    Mayonnaise, 132–33

  Grilled Zucchini Succotash,
    38–39

  heat scale, 19

  Lamb Burgers with Tomato-Mint
    Salsa and Feta Cheese,
    172–73

  Pickled Jalapeños, 58–59

  Pork Tenderloin Crusted with
    Green Onion, Jalapeño, and
    Ginger, 144–45

  roasting, 25

  Smoky and Fiery Skirt Steak with
    Avocado-Oregano Relish,
    166–67

  Souvlaki with Merguez Sausage
    and Piquillo Pepper–Yogurt
    Sauce, 174–76

  types of, 17–19

  Whole Sea Bass with Charred
    Serrano–Basil Vinaigrette,
    104–5

chimney starter, 7–8

Chinese Chicken Salad with Red
  Chile–Peanut Dressing,
  126–27

chives, 13–14

  Cumin Grilled Sea Scallops with
    Chickpea Salad and Red
    Pepper–Tahini Vinaigrette,
    80–82

  Grilled New Potatoes with
    Lemon-Garlic Aïoli and
    Chives, 56–57

chives (*cont.*)

  Grilled Portobello Mushrooms
    Stacked with Spinach and
    Manchego Cheese, 46–47

chocolate, Grilled Apricots with
  Bittersweet Chocolate and
  Almonds, 186

cilantro, 14

  "Barbecued" Mahimahi with
    Yellow Pepper–Cilantro Pesto,
    88–89

  Buckwheat Pizza with Cilantro
    Pesto, Jack Cheese, and
    Grilled Shrimp, 62–64

  Chinese Chicken Salad with
    Red Chile–Peanut Dressing,
    126–27

  Grilled Chicken Breasts Stuffed
    with Goat Cheese with Green
    Chile–Cilantro Sauce, 124–25

  Grilled Oysters with Mango Pico
    de Gallo and Red Chile
    Horseradish, 78–79

  Grilled Prawns with Spicy Fresh
    Pepper Sauce, 68–69

  Grilled Sea Scallops with
    Avocado Vinaigrette and
    Jalapeño Pesto, 84–85

  Grilled Shrimp Escabeche,
    72–73

  Grilled Tuna with Fennel-
    Tomatillo Relish, 112–13

  Grilled Turkey Burgers with
    Monterey Jack, Poblano Pickle
    Relish, and Avocado
    Mayonnaise, 132–33

  Grilled Zucchini Succotash,
    38–39

  Pickled Jalapeños, 58–59

  Red Cabbage and Beet Slaw,
    48–49

  Smoky and Fiery Skirt Steak with
    Avocado-Oregano Relish,
    166–67

cinnamon, 15

citrus. *See* grapefruit; lemons;
  limes; oranges

Clams, Grilled, on the Half-Shell
  with Bacon, Garlic, and Hot
  Pepper, 76–77

coals, heating, 6

coconut milk, Pork Satay with Red
  Chile–Peanut Sauce and Napa
  Cabbage–Green Onion Slaw,
  148–50

coffee grinders, electric, 9

coriander, 15

  Espresso-Rubbed BBQ Ribs with
    Mustard-Vinegar Basting
    Sauce, 151–53

  Grilled Duck Breast with Black
    Pepper–Sweet Mustard Sauce,
    140–41

  Grilled Jerk-Rubbed Grouper
    with Hot Vinegar Sauce,
    94–95

  Grilled Spice-Rubbed Vidalia
    Onions, 52–53

  Grilled Turkey Cutlets and Sage-
    Lemon Pesto, 134–35

corn, Grilled Zucchini Succotash,
  38–39

cornichons, 24

  Grilled Asparagus and Egg
    Salad with Tarragon-Caper
    Vinaigrette, 30–31

crème fraîche, 21

  Grilled Figs with Vanilla-Orange
    Crème Fraîche and Toasted
    Pistachios, 190–91

cucumbers, Greek Orzo and
  Grilled Shrimp Salad with
  Mustard-Dill Vinaigrette,
  70–71

cumin, 15

  "Barbecued" Mahimahi with
    Yellow Pepper–Cilantro Pesto,
    88–89

  Cumin Grilled Sea Scallops with
    Chickpea Salad and Red
    Pepper–Tahini Vinaigrette,
    80–82

  Grilled Spice-Rubbed Vidalia
    Onions, 52–53

  Spanish-Spiced Chicken with
    Mustard–Green Onion Sauce,
    128–29

desserts

  Grilled Apricots with
    Bittersweet Chocolate and
    Almonds, 186

  Grilled Figs with Vanilla-Orange
    Crème Fraîche and Toasted
    Pistachios, 190–91

  Grilled Plums with Spiced
    Walnut-Yogurt Sauce,
    188–89

  Strawberries with Ricotta Cream,
    187

dill, 14
  Greek Orzo and Grilled Shrimp
    Salad with Mustard-Dill
    Vinaigrette, 70–71
  Grilled Salmon with Lemon,
    Dill, and Caper Vinaigrette,
    102–3
dill pickles, Grilled Turkey Burgers
    with Monterey Jack, Poblano
    Pickle Relish, and Avocado
    Mayonnaise, 132–33
drinks
  Cantaloupe-Mint Agua Fresca
    (Mexican Fruit Cooler), 182
  Green Tea Mint Iced Tea, 183
  Pomegranate Margarita, 184
  White Nectarine Bellini, 185
duck
  Balsamic-Thyme-Glazed Duck
    Breasts, 138–39
  Grilled Duck Breast with Black
    Pepper–Sweet Mustard Sauce,
    140–41

eggplant
  Grilled Antipasto with
    Gorgonzola Vinaigrette, 32–33
  Grilled Asian-Style Eggplant
    Salad, 36–37
  Grilled Halibut with Grilled
    Eggplant Salad, 90–91
eggs
  Grilled Asparagus and Egg
    Salad with Tarragon-Caper
    Vinaigrette, 30–31
  hard-cooked, 118
  Tuna au Poivre Salad with
    Creamy Tarragon-Garlic
    Vinaigrette, 116–17
electric coffee grinders, 9
Escabeche, Grilled Shrimp, 72–73
Espresso-Rubbed BBQ Ribs with
    Mustard-Vinegar Basting
    Sauce, 151–53

farro, Harissa-Marinated Lamb
    Skewers on Farro Salad with
    Pine Nuts and Goat Cheese,
    168–69
fennel
  Grilled Fennel and Orange
    Salad with Almonds and Mint,
    40–41
  Grilled Tuna with Fennel-
    Tomatillo Relish, 112–13

fennel seeds
  Grilled Fennel-Spiced Pork
    Chops with Sage-Lemon
    Vinaigrette, 146–47
  Grilled Jerk-Rubbed Grouper
    with Hot Vinegar Sauce,
    94–95
  Grilled Tuna with Fennel-
    Tomatillo Relish, 112–13
  Spanish-Spiced Chicken with
    Mustard–Green Onion Sauce,
    128–29
Figs, Grilled, with Vanilla-Orange
    Crème Fraîche and Toasted
    Pistachios, 190–91

garlic, 23
  Bricked Rosemary Chicken with
    Lemon, 136–37
  Garlic-Mustard-Grilled Beef
    Skewers, 154–55
  Garlic–Red Chile–Thyme–
    Marinated Shrimp, 66–67
  Grilled Asian-Style Eggplant
    Salad, 36–37
  Grilled New Potatoes with
    Lemon-Garlic Aïoli and
    Chives, 56–57
  Grilled T-Bone Steaks with
    Garlic-Chile Oil, 162–63
  roasting, 25
gas grills, 7
ginger
  Chinese Chicken Salad with Red
    Chile–Peanut Dressing, 126–27
  Grilled Jerk-Rubbed Grouper
    with Hot Vinegar Sauce,
    94–95
  Grilled Lobster Tails with Hot
    Ginger–Green Onion
    Vinaigrette, 86–87
  Grilled Shrimp in Lettuce Leaves
    with Serrano–Mint Sauce,
    74–75
  Pork Satay with Red Chile–
    Peanut Sauce and Napa
    Cabbage–Green Onion Slaw,
    148–50
  Pork Tenderloin Crusted with
    Green Onion, Jalapeño, and
    Ginger, 144–45
grapefruit, 24
  Grilled Red Snapper with
    Grapefruit-Thyme Mojo,
    96–97

grapefruit (cont.)
  grilling, 26
  segmenting, 26
Greek Orzo and Grilled Shrimp
    Salad with Mustard-Dill
    Vinaigrette, 70–71
Greek yogurt, 21
  Dipping Sauce, 130–31
  Grilled Chicken Tenders with
    Spicy Chipotle Sauce and Blue
    Cheese–Yogurt
  Grilled Lamb Chops and
    Oregano Vinaigrette with
    Radish Tzatziki, 170–71
  Grilled Plums with Spiced
    Walnut-Yogurt Sauce,
    188–89
  Souvlaki with Merguez Sausage
    and Piquillo Pepper–Yogurt
    Sauce, 174–76
  Yogurt-Mint-Marinated Grilled
    Leg of Lamb, 178–79
green beans, Tuna au Poivre Salad
    with Creamy Tarragon-Garlic
    Vinaigrette, 116–17
Green Chile Burgers, 156–57
green onions
  Bulgur Salad with Green Onion
    Vinaigrette, 50–51
  Chinese Chicken Salad with Red
    Chile–Peanut Dressing,
    126–27
  Greek Orzo and Grilled Shrimp
    Salad with Mustard-Dill
    Vinaigrette, 70–71
  Grilled Lobster Tails with Hot
    Ginger–Green Onion
    Vinaigrette, 86–87
  Grilled Tuna Burgers with Green
    Onion Mayonnaise and
    Watercress, 114–15
  Pork Satay with Red Chile–
    Peanut Sauce and Napa
    Cabbage–Green Onion Slaw,
    148–50
  Pork Tenderloin Crusted with
    Green Onion, Jalapeño, and
    Ginger, 144–45
  Spanish-Spiced Chicken with
    Mustard–Green Onion Sauce,
    128–29
  Yucatán Marinated Halibut in
    Banana Leaves with
    Pineapple-Orange Relish,
    92–93

Green Tea Mint Iced Tea, 183
Grilled and Marinated Zucchini
  and Yellow Squash, 34–35
Grilled Antipasto with Gorgonzola
  Vinaigrette, 32–33
Grilled Apricots with Bittersweet
  Chocolate and Almonds, 186
Grilled Asian-Style Eggplant
  Salad, 36–37
Grilled Asparagus and Egg Salad
  with Tarragon-Caper
  Vinaigrette, 30–31
Grilled Beef Filet with Arugula and
  Parmesan, 160–61
Grilled Brook Trout with
  Horseradish and Tarragon
  Tartar Sauce, 106–7
Grilled Chicken Breasts with
  Fontina and Prosciutto with
  Sage-Orange Vinaigrette,
  122–23
Grilled Chicken Breasts Stuffed
  with Goat Cheese with Green
  Chile–Cilantro Sauce, 124–25
Grilled Chicken Cutlets with
  Lemon and Black Pepper and
  Arugula-Tomato Salad, 120–21
Grilled Chicken Tenders with
  Spicy Chipotle Sauce and
  Blue Cheese–Yogurt Sauce,
  130–31
Grilled Clams on the Half-Shell
  with Bacon, Garlic, and Hot
  Pepper, 76–77
Grilled Duck Breast with Black
  Pepper–Sweet Mustard Sauce,
  140–41
Grilled Fennel and Orange Salad
  with Almonds and Mint,
  40–41
Grilled Fennel-Spiced Pork Chops
  with Sage-Lemon Vinaigrette,
  146–47
Grilled Figs with Vanilla-Orange
  Crème Fraîche and Toasted
  Pistachios, 190–91
Grilled German Sweet Potato
  Salad, 42–43
Grilled Halibut with Grilled
  Eggplant Salad, 90–91
Grilled Jerk-Rubbed Grouper with
  Hot Vinegar Sauce, 94–95
Grilled Lamb Chops and Oregano
  Vinaigrette with Radish
  Tzatziki, 170–71

Grilled Lobster Tails with Hot
  Ginger–Green Onion Vinai-
  grette, 86–87
Grilled New Potatoes with
  Lemon-Garlic Aïoli and
  Chives, 56–57
Grilled Oysters with Mango Pico
  de Gallo and Red Chile
  Horseradish, 78–79
Grilled Plums with Spiced Walnut-
  Yogurt Sauce, 188–89
Grilled Portobello Mushrooms
  Stacked with Spinach and
  Manchego Cheese, 46–47
Grilled Prawns with Spicy Fresh
  Pepper Sauce, 68–69
Grilled Red Snapper with
  Grapefruit-Thyme Mojo, 96–97
Grilled Red Snapper with Green
  Romesco Sauce, 98–99
Grilled Salmon with Anchovy
  Vinaigrette and Grilled
  Pepper and Black Olive
  Relish, 100–101
Grilled Salmon with Lemon, Dill,
  and Caper Vinaigrette, 102–3
Grilled Sea Scallops with Avocado
  Vinaigrette and Jalapeño
  Pesto, 84–85
Grilled Shrimp Escabeche,
  72–73
Grilled Shrimp in Lettuce Leaves
  with Serrano–Mint Sauce,
  74–75
Grilled Spice-Rubbed Vidalia
  Onions, 52–53
Grilled Sweet Potato Salad with
  Pancetta and Rosemary
  Vinaigrette, 44–45
Grilled T-Bone Steaks with Garlic-
  Chile Oil, 162–63
Grilled Tuna Burgers with Green
  Onion Mayonnaise and
  Watercress, 114–15
Grilled Tuna Salad Sandwiches
  with Lemon-Habanero
  Mayonnaise, 110–11
Grilled Tuna with Fennel-Tomatillo
  Relish, 112–13
Grilled Tuna with White Bean
  Salad, 108–9
Grilled Turkey Burgers with
  Monterey Jack, Poblano Pickle
  Relish, and Avocado
  Mayonnaise, 132–33

Grilled Turkey Cutlets and Sage-
  Lemon Pesto, 134–35
Grilled Zucchini Succotash, 38–39
grills
  cleaning, 8
  heating coals for, 6
  types of, 7
Grouper, Grilled Jerk-Rubbed,
  with Hot Vinegar Sauce,,
  94–95

halibut
  Grilled Halibut with Grilled
    Eggplant Salad, 90–91
  Yucatán Marinated Halibut in
    Banana Leaves with
    Pineapple-Orange Relish,
    92–93
Harissa-Marinated Lamb Skewers
  on Farro Salad with Pine Nuts
  and Goat Cheese, 168–69
herbs
  types of, 13–15
  See also specific herbs
honey, 22
  Garlic-Mustard-Grilled Beef
    Skewers, 154–55
  Grilled Halibut with Grilled
    Eggplant Salad, 90–91
horseradish
  Grilled Brook Trout with
    Horseradish and Tarragon
    Tartar Sauce, 106–7
  Grilled Oysters with Mango Pico
    de Gallo and Red Chile
    Horseradish, 78–79
  Red Cabbage and Beet Slaw,
    48–49

lamb
  Grilled Lamb Chops and
    Oregano Vinaigrette with
    Radish Tzatziki, 170–71
  Harissa-Marinated Lamb
    Skewers on Farro Salad with
    Pine Nuts and Goat Cheese,
    168–69
  Lamb Burgers with Tomato-
    Mint Salsa and Feta Cheese,
    172–73
  Souvlaki with Merguez Sausage
    and Piquillo Pepper–Yogurt
    Sauce, 174–76
  Yogurt-Mint-Marinated Grilled
    Leg of Lamb, 178–79

lemons, 24
  Bricked Rosemary Chicken with Lemon, 136–37
  Grilled and Marinated Zucchini and Yellow Squash, 34–35
  Grilled Chicken Cutlets with Lemon and Black Pepper and Arugula-Tomato Salad, 120–21
  Grilled Fennel-Spiced Pork Chops with Sage-Lemon Vinaigrette, 146–47
  Grilled New Potatoes with Lemon-Garlic Aïoli and Chives, 56–57
  Grilled Salmon with Lemon, Dill, and Caper Vinaigrette, 102–3
  Grilled Tuna Salad Sandwiches with Lemon-Habanero Mayonnaise, 110–11
  Grilled Tuna with Fennel-Tomatillo Relish, 112–13
  Grilled Turkey Cutlets and Sage-Lemon Pesto, 134–35
  grilling, 26
  Red Wine–Rosemary–Marinated Flank Steak with Lemony White Beans, 164–65
  Souvlaki with Merguez Sausage and Piquillo Pepper–Yogurt Sauce, 174–76
  Yucatán Marinated Halibut in Banana Leaves with Pineapple-Orange Relish, 92–93
lettuce
  Chinese Chicken Salad with Red Chile–Peanut Dressing, 126–27
  Grilled Shrimp in Lettuce Leaves with Serrano–Mint Sauce, 74–75
lima beans, Grilled Zucchini Succotash, 38–39
limes, 24
  Bulgur Salad with Green Onion Vinaigrette, 50–51
  Grilled Chicken Breasts Stuffed with Goat Cheese with Green Chile–Cilantro Sauce, 124–25
  Grilled Oysters with Mango Pico de Gallo and Red Chile Horseradish, 78–79

limes (*cont.*)
  Grilled Sea Scallops with Avocado Vinaigrette and Jalapeño Pesto, 84–85
  Grilled Shrimp in Lettuce Leaves with Serrano–Mint Sauce, 74–75
  Grilled Tuna Burgers with Green Onion Mayonnaise and Watercress, 114–15
  Grilled Turkey Burgers with Monterey Jack, Poblano Pickle Relish, and Avocado Mayonnaise, 132–33
  grilling, 26
  Lamb Burgers with Tomato-Mint Salsa and Feta Cheese, 172–73
  Pomegranate Margarita, 184
  Pork Satay with Red Chile–Peanut Sauce and Napa Cabbage–Green Onion Slaw, 148–50
  Pork Tenderloin Crusted with Green Onion, Jalapeño, and Ginger, 144–45
  Smoky and Fiery Skirt Steak with Avocado-Oregano Relish, 166–67
  Yucatán Marinated Halibut in Banana Leaves with Pineapple-Orange Relish, 92–93
  Lobster, Grilled Tails with Hot Ginger–Green Onion Vinaigrette, 86–87

Mahimahi, "Barbecued," with Yellow Pepper–Cilantro Pesto, 88–89
mango, Grilled Oysters with Mango Pico de Gallo and Red Chile Horseradish, 78–79
Margarita, Pomegranate, 184
mayonnaise
  Grilled New Potatoes with Lemon-Garlic Aïoli and Chives, 56–57
  Grilled Tuna Burgers with Green Onion Mayonnaise and Watercress, 114–15
  Grilled Tuna Salad Sandwiches with Lemon-Habanero Mayonnaise, 110–11

mayonnaise (*cont.*)
  Grilled Turkey Burgers with Monterey Jack, Poblano Pickle Relish, and Avocado Mayonnaise, 132–33
mint, 14
  Bulgur Salad with Green Onion Vinaigrette, 50–51
  Cantaloupe-Mint Agua Fresca (Mexican Fruit Cooler), 182
  Green Tea Mint Iced Tea, 183
  Grilled Fennel and Orange Salad with Almonds and Mint, 40–41
  Grilled Shrimp in Lettuce Leaves with Serrano–Mint Sauce, 74–75
  Harissa-Marinated Lamb Skewers on Farro Salad with Pine Nuts and Goat Cheese, 168–69
  Lamb Burgers with Tomato-Mint Salsa and Feta Cheese, 172–73
  Red Wine–Rosemary–Marinated Flank Steak with Lemony White Beans, 164–65
  Yogurt-Mint-Marinated Grilled Leg of Lamb, 178–79
  Yucatán Marinated Halibut in Banana Leaves with Pineapple-Orange Relish, 92–93
mushrooms. *See* portobello mushrooms
mustard
  Espresso-Rubbed BBQ Ribs with Mustard-Vinegar Basting Sauce, 151–53
  Garlic-Mustard-Grilled Beef Skewers, 154–55
  Greek Orzo and Grilled Shrimp Salad with Mustard-Dill Vinaigrette, 70–71
  Grilled Chicken Tenders with Spicy Chipotle Sauce and Blue Cheese–Yogurt Sauce, 130–31
  Grilled Duck Breast with Black Pepper–Sweet Mustard Sauce, 140–41
  Grilled German Sweet Potato Salad, 42–43
  Grilled Portobello Mushrooms Stacked with Spinach and Manchego Cheese, 46–47

mustard (*cont.*)
Grilled Salmon with Anchovy Vinaigrette and Grilled Pepper and Black Olive Relish, 100–101
Grilled Tuna Burgers with Green Onion Mayonnaise and Watercress, 114–15
Spanish-Spiced Chicken with Mustard–Green Onion Sauce, 128–29
Whole Sea Bass with Charred Serrano–Basil Vinaigrette, 104–5

nectarines, White Nectarine Bellini, 185
nuts. *See* peanut butter; pine nuts; pistachios; walnuts
nuts, toasting, 26

oils, types of, 23
olives
Grilled Antipasto with Gorgonzola Vinaigrette, 32–33
Grilled Chicken Breasts Stuffed with Goat Cheese with Green Chile–Cilantro Sauce, 124–25
Grilled Halibut with Grilled Eggplant Salad, 90–91
Grilled Salmon with Anchovy Vinaigrette and Grilled Pepper and Black Olive Relish, 100–101
Grilled Shrimp Escabeche, 72–73
Tuna au Poivre Salad with Creamy Tarragon-Garlic Vinaigrette, 116–17
onions, 23
Grilled Spice-Rubbed Vidalia Onions, 52–53
grilling, 25
See also green onions
oranges, 24
Grilled Chicken Breasts with Fontina and Prosciutto with Sage-Orange Vinaigrette, 122–23
Grilled Fennel and Orange Salad with Almonds and Mint, 40–41
Grilled Figs with Vanilla-Orange Crème Fraîche and Toasted Pistachios, 190–91

oranges (*cont.*)
Grilled Plums with Spiced Walnut-Yogurt Sauce, 188–89
Grilled Red Snapper with Grapefruit-Thyme Mojo, 96–97
grilling, 26
segmenting, 26
Yucatán Marinated Halibut in Banana Leaves with Pineapple-Orange Relish, 92–93
oregano, 14
Grilled Lamb Chops and Oregano Vinaigrette with Radish Tzatziki, 170–71
Oysters, Grilled, with Mango Pico de Gallo and Red Chile Horseradish, 78–79

pancetta, Grilled Sweet Potato Salad with Pancetta and Rosemary Vinaigrette, 44–45
paprika, 16
"Barbecued" Mahimahi with Yellow Pepper–Cilantro Pesto, 88–89
Espresso-Rubbed BBQ Ribs with Mustard-Vinegar Basting Sauce, 151–53
Garlic-Mustard-Grilled Beef Skewers, 154–55
Grilled Red Snapper with Green Romesco Sauce, 98–99
Spanish-Spiced Chicken with Mustard–Green Onion Sauce, 128–29
parsley, 14
Buckwheat Pizza with Cilantro Pesto, Jack Cheese, and Grilled Shrimp, 62–64
Bulgur Salad with Green Onion Vinaigrette, 50–51
Cumin Grilled Sea Scallops with Chickpea Salad and Red Pepper–Tahini Vinaigrette, 80–82
Grilled Clams on the Half-Shell with Bacon, Garlic, and Hot Pepper, 76–77
Grilled Halibut with Grilled Eggplant Salad, 90–91
Grilled Jerk-Rubbed Grouper with Hot Vinegar Sauce, 94–95

parsley (*cont.*)
Grilled Red Snapper with Green Romesco Sauce, 98–99
Grilled Salmon with Anchovy Vinaigrette and Grilled Pepper and Black Olive Relish, 100–101
Grilled Tuna with White Bean Salad, 108–9
Grilled Turkey Cutlets and Sage-Lemon Pesto, 134–35
Pork Satay with Red Chile–Peanut Sauce and Napa Cabbage–Green Onion Slaw, 148–50
Red Wine–Rosemary–Marinated Flank Steak with Lemony White Beans, 164–65
Spanish-Spiced Chicken with Mustard–Green Onion Sauce, 128–29
peanut butter
Chinese Chicken Salad with Red Chile–Peanut Dressing, 126–27
Pork Satay with Red Chile–Peanut Sauce and Napa Cabbage–Green Onion Slaw, 148–50
pepper, black, 16
peppers. *See* bell peppers; chiles
Pickled Jalapeños, 58–59
pineapple, Yucatán Marinated Halibut in Banana Leaves with Pineapple-Orange Relish, 92–93
pine nuts
"Barbecued" Mahimahi with Yellow Pepper–Cilantro Pesto, 88–89
Black Pepper–Crusted Filet Mignon with Goat Cheese and Roasted Red Pepper–Ancho Salsa, 158–59
Grilled Halibut with Grilled Eggplant Salad, 90–91
Grilled Sea Scallops with Avocado Vinaigrette and Jalapeño Pesto, 84–85
Harissa-Marinated Lamb Skewers on Farro Salad with Pine Nuts and Goat Cheese, 168–69

pistachios, Pork Satay with Red Chile–Peanut Sauce and Napa Cabbage–Green Onion Slaw, 148–50

Pizza, Buckwheat, with Cilantro Pesto, Jack Cheese, and Grilled Shrimp, 62–64

Plums, Grilled, with Spiced Walnut-Yogurt Sauce, 188–89

Pomegranate Margarita, 184

pork
Espresso-Rubbed BBQ Ribs with Mustard-Vinegar Basting Sauce, 151–53
Grilled Fennel-Spiced Pork Chops with Sage-Lemon Vinaigrette, 146–47
Pork Satay with Red Chile–Peanut Sauce and Napa Cabbage–Green Onion Slaw, 148–50
Pork Tenderloin Crusted with Green Onion, Jalapeño, and Ginger, 144–45

portobello mushrooms
Grilled Antipasto with Gorgonzola Vinaigrette, 32–33
Grilled Portobello Mushrooms Stacked with Spinach and Manchego Cheese, 46–47

Potatoes, Grilled New, with Lemon-Garlic Aïoli and Chives, 56–57

prawns
Grilled Prawns with Spicy Fresh Pepper Sauce, 68–69
See also shrimp

prosciutto, Grilled Chicken Breasts Filled with Fontina and with Sage-Orange Vinaigrette, 122–23

pumpkin seeds, Buckwheat Pizza with Cilantro Pesto, Jack Cheese, and Grilled Shrimp, 62–64

radicchio, Grilled Tuna with White Bean Salad, 108–9

radishes
Grilled Lamb Chops and Oregano Vinaigrette with Radish Tzatziki, 170–71
Grilled Shrimp Escabeche, 72–73

raisins, Grilled Halibut with Grilled Eggplant Salad, 90–91

Red Cabbage and Beet Slaw, 48–49

red snapper
Grilled Red Snapper with Grapefruit-Thyme Mojo, 96–97
Grilled Red Snapper with Green Romesco Sauce, 98–99

Red Wine–Rosemary–Marinated Flank Steak with Lemony White Beans, 164–65

rosemary, 14
Bricked Rosemary Chicken with Lemon, 136–37
Grilled Sweet Potato Salad with Pancetta and Rosemary Vinaigrette, 44–45
Red Wine–Rosemary–Marinated Flank Steak with Lemony White Beans, 164–65

sage, 14–15
Grilled Chicken Breasts with Fontina and Prosciutto with Sage-Orange Vinaigrette, 122–23
Grilled Fennel-Spiced Pork Chops with Sage-Lemon Vinaigrette, 146–47
Grilled Turkey Cutlets and Sage-Lemon Pesto, 134–35

salads
Bulgur Salad with Green Onion Vinaigrette, 50–51
Chinese Chicken Salad with Red Chile–Peanut Dressing, 126–27
Cumin Grilled Sea Scallops with Chickpea Salad and Red Pepper–Tahini Vinaigrette, 80–82
Greek Orzo and Grilled Shrimp Salad with Mustard-Dill Vinaigrette, 70–71
Grilled Asian-Style Eggplant Salad, 36–37
Grilled Asparagus and Egg Salad with Tarragon-Caper Vinaigrette, 30–31
Grilled Chicken Cutlets with Lemon and Black Pepper and Arugula-Tomato Salad, 120–21
Grilled Fennel and Orange Salad with Almonds and Mint, 40–41

salads (cont.)
Grilled Halibut with Grilled Eggplant Salad, 90–91
Grilled Sweet Potato Salad with Pancetta and Rosemary Vinaigrette, 44–45
Grilled Tuna with White Bean Salad, 108–9
Harissa-Marinated Lamb Skewers on Farro Salad with Pine Nuts and Goat Cheese, 168–69
Pork Satay with Red Chile–Peanut Sauce and Napa Cabbage–Green Onion Slaw, 148–50
Red Cabbage and Beet Slaw, 48–49
Tuna au Poivre Salad with Creamy Tarragon-Garlic Vinaigrette, 116–17

salmon
Grilled Salmon with Anchovy Vinaigrette and Grilled Pepper and Black Olive Relish, 100–101
Grilled Salmon with Lemon, Dill, and Caper Vinaigrette, 102–3

salt, 16

sandwiches
Green Chile Burgers, 156–57
Grilled Tuna Burgers with Green Onion Mayonnaise and Watercress, 114–15
Grilled Tuna Salad Sandwiches with Lemon-Habanero Mayonnaise, 110–11
Grilled Turkey Burgers with Monterey Jack, Poblano Pickle Relish, and Avocado Mayonnaise, 132–33
Lamb Burgers with Tomato-Mint Salsa and Feta Cheese, 172–73

sausage, Souvlaki with Merguez Sausage and Piquillo Pepper–Yogurt Sauce, 174–76

scallions. See green onions

scallops
Cumin Grilled Sea Scallops with Chickpea Salad and Red Pepper–Tahini Vinaigrette, 80–82

scallops (*cont.*)
Grilled Sea Scallops with
Avocado Vinaigrette and
Jalapeño Pesto, 84–85
Sea bass, Whole, with Charred
Serrano–Basil Vinaigrette,
104–5
seeds
toasting, 26
See also fennel seeds; pumpkin
seeds; sesame seeds
sesame seeds, Grilled Lobster Tails
with Hot Ginger–Green Onion
Vinaigrette, 86–87
shallots
Grilled Portobello Mushrooms
Stacked with Spinach and
Manchego Cheese, 46–47
Grilled Salmon with Anchovy
Vinaigrette and Grilled
Pepper and Black Olive
Relish, 100–101
Grilled Sweet Potato Salad with
Pancetta and Rosemary
Vinaigrette, 44–45
Pork Satay with Red Chile–
Peanut Sauce and Napa
Cabbage–Green Onion Slaw,
148–50
shrimp
Buckwheat Pizza with Cilantro
Pesto, Jack Cheese, and
Grilled Shrimp, 62–64
Garlic–Red Chile–Thyme–
Marinated Shrimp, 66–67
Greek Orzo and Grilled Shrimp
Salad with Mustard-Dill
Vinaigrette, 70–71
Grilled Prawns with Spicy Fresh
Pepper Sauce, 68–69
Grilled Shrimp Escabeche,
72–73
Grilled Shrimp in Lettuce Leaves
with Serrano–Mint Sauce, 74–75
sizes, 65
skewers
Garlic-Mustard-Grilled Beef
Skewers, 154–55
Grilled Lobster Tails with Hot
Ginger–Green Onion
Vinaigrette, 86–87
Harissa-Marinated Lamb
Skewers on Farro Salad with
Pine Nuts and Goat Cheese,
168–69

skewers (*cont.*)
Pork Satay with Red Chile–
Peanut Sauce and Napa
Cabbage–Green Onion Slaw,
148–50
types of, 87
Smoky and Fiery Skirt Steak with
Avocado-Oregano Relish,
166–67
snow peas, Chinese Chicken Salad
with Red Chile–Peanut
Dressing, 126–27
Souvlaki with Merguez Sausage
and Piquillo Pepper–Yogurt
Sauce, 174–76
soy sauce
Garlic-Mustard-Grilled Beef
Skewers, 154–55
Grilled Asian-Style Eggplant
Salad, 36–37
Grilled Lobster Tails with Hot
Ginger–Green Onion
Vinaigrette, 86–87
Grilled Shrimp in Lettuce
Leaves with Serrano–Mint
Sauce, 74–75
Pork Satay with Red Chile–
Peanut Sauce and Napa
Cabbage–Green Onion Slaw,
148–50
Pork Tenderloin Crusted with
Green Onion, Jalapeño, and
Ginger, 144–45
Spanish-Spiced Chicken with
Mustard–Green Onion Sauce,
128–29
spatulas, 9
spices
toasting, 26
types of, 15–16
See also specific spices
spinach, Grilled Portobello
Mushrooms Stacked with
Spinach and Manchego
Cheese, 46–47
squeeze bottles, 9–10
Strawberries with Ricotta Cream,
187
Succotash, Grilled Zucchini, 38–39
sweet potatoes
Grilled German Sweet Potato
Salad, 42–43
Grilled Sweet Potato Salad with
Pancetta and Rosemary
Vinaigrette, 44–45

tahini, 24
Cumin Grilled Sea Scallops with
Chickpea Salad and Red
Pepper–Tahini Vinaigrette,
80–82
Red Wine–Rosemary–
Marinated Flank Steak with
Lemony White Beans, 164–65
tarragon, 15
Grilled Asparagus and Egg
Salad with Tarragon-Caper
Vinaigrette, 30–31
Grilled Brook Trout with
Horseradish and Tarragon
Tartar Sauce, 106–7
tea, Green Tea Mint Iced Tea,
183
temperatures
for grilling specific foods,
11–12
thermometers and, 9, 11
tequila, Pomegranate Margarita,
184
thermometers, meat, 9, 11
thyme, 15
Balsamic-Thyme-Glazed Duck
Breasts, 138–39
Garlic–Red Chile–Thyme–
Marinated Shrimp, 66–67
Grilled Antipasto with Gor-
gonzola Vinaigrette, 32–33
Grilled Chicken Breasts Stuffed
with Goat Cheese with Green
Chile–Cilantro Sauce, 124–25
Grilled Duck Breast with Black
Pepper–Sweet Mustard Sauce,
140–41
Grilled German Sweet Potato
Salad, 42–43
Grilled Jerk-Rubbed Grouper
with Hot Vinegar Sauce, 94–95
Grilled Red Snapper with
Grapefruit-Thyme Mojo, 96–97
Grilled Salmon with Anchovy
Vinaigrette and Grilled
Pepper and Black Olive Rel-
ish, 100–101
Grilled T-Bone Steaks with
Garlic-Chile Oil, 162–63
Red Wine–Rosemary–
Marinated Flank Steak with
Lemony White Beans, 164–65
tomatillos, Grilled Tuna with
Fennel-Tomatillo Relish,
112–13

tomatoes
  Bulgur Salad with Green Onion
    Vinaigrette, 50–51
  Greek Orzo and Grilled Shrimp
    Salad with Mustard-Dill
    Vinaigrette, 70–71
  Green Chile Burgers, 156–57
  Grilled Chicken Cutlets with
    Lemon and Black Pepper and
    Arugula-Tomato Salad, 120–21
  Grilled Halibut with Grilled
    Eggplant Salad, 90–91
  Grilled Zucchini Succotash,
    38–39
  Lamb Burgers with Tomato-
    Mint Salsa and Feta Cheese,
    172–73
tongs, 8
towels, 10
trout, Grilled Brook Trout with
    Horseradish and Tarragon
    Tartar Sauce, 106–7
tuna
  Grilled Tuna Burgers with Green
    Onion Mayonnaise and
    Watercress, 114–15
  Grilled Tuna Salad Sandwiches
    with Lemon-Habanero
    Mayonnaise, 110–11
  Grilled Tuna with Fennel-
    Tomatillo Relish, 112–13
  Grilled Tuna with White Bean
    Salad, 108–9

tuna (cont.)
  Tuna au Poivre Salad with
    Creamy Tarragon-Garlic
    Vinaigrette, 116–17
turkey
  Grilled Turkey Burgers with
    Monterey Jack, Poblano Pickle
    Relish, and Avocado
    Mayonnaise, 132–33
  Grilled Turkey Cutlets and
    Sage-Lemon Pesto, 134–35
  Twice-Grilled Peppers with Buffalo
    Mozzarella and Caper-Basil
    Vinaigrette, 54–55

vinegar, types of, 22

walnuts, Grilled Plums with Spiced
    Walnut-Yogurt Sauce, 188–89
watercress
  Grilled Tuna Burgers with Green
    Onion Mayonnaise and
    Watercress, 114–15
  Grilled Tuna Salad Sandwiches
    with Lemon-Habanero
    Mayonnaise, 110–11
white beans
  Grilled Tuna with White Bean
    Salad, 108–9
  Red Wine–Rosemary–
    Marinated Flank Steak with
    Lemony White Beans,
    164–65

White Nectarine Bellini, 185
Whole Sea Bass with Charred
    Serrano–Basil Vinaigrette,
    104–5
wine
  Red Wine–Rosemary–
    Marinated Flank Steak
    with Lemony White Beans,
    164–65
  White Nectarine Bellini,
    185

yellow squash
  Grilled and Marinated
    Zucchini and Yellow Squash,
    34–35
  Grilled Antipasto with
    Gorgonzola Vinaigrette,
    32–33
yogurt. See Greek yogurt
Yogurt-Mint-Marinated Grilled
    Leg of Lamb, 178–79
Yucatán Marinated Halibut in
    Banana Leaves with
    Pineapple-Orange Relish,
    92–93

zucchini
  Grilled and Marinated
    Zucchini and Yellow Squash,
    34–35
  Grilled Zucchini Succotash,
    38–39